WORKING

UP A PART

A Manual for the Beginning Actor

BY H. D. ALBRIGHT, CORNELL UNIVERSITY

HOUGHTON MIFFLIN COMPANY · Boston · New York

Chicago · Dallas · Atlanta · San Francisco · The Riverside Press Cambridge

The Riverside Press

CAMBRIDGE · MASSACHUSETTS

PRINTED IN THE U.S.A.

TO

James Albert Winans

AND THOSE WHO CAME AFTER

Contents

★★★───★★★

List of Illustrations

✦✦✦ ─────────────────────────────── ✦✦✦

Preface

✱✱✱————————————————————————————————✱✱✱

THIS MANUAL is primarily intended to serve as: a) a textbook for college classes in acting; b) a handbook for those actors in school or community who may have begun to "act," in the sense that they have already been cast in several parts, but who have had no real training and wish practical assistance in preparing a role of some proportions. In either case, the manual is meant for *the beginner* — before he has read widely in more advanced works, or at least before he has developed from wide reading and experience a workable system of his own.

In keeping with both of these aims, the volume offers a brief though not superficial introduction to the many inter-related problems of play presentation, as the actor must sooner or later face them. The seasoned student-actor who has had even a minimum of formal training can of course be expected to bring to his work some knowledge of the broader problems of production, and some awareness of the director's aims and responsibilities. The experienced player has already struggled with his own voice and speech, his own posture and movement; he has already faced the complications of dramatic structure, characterization, audience psychology. But all of these, and more, crowd in on the beginner at once.

It is unlikely that any single volume, indeed any single class or laboratory, will neatly solve all his problems immediately. *Working Up A Part*, however, does attempt to outline a sound and practical approach for the beginner. Moving from analysis of a role, through rehearsal, to performance, it presents an orderly, logical, and balanced arrangement of material. No one aspect of the beginner's task is slighted at the expense of others; and the material is so organized that the volume may readily be used either as a basic class text or as a reference handbook.

At the end of the main chapters, check-lists of questions for testing the actor's progress are included; and these are supplemented throughout by exercises and drills. Ten scenes for rehearsal and informal presentation are included in an appendix. Varying widely in mood and content, and planned for both men and women, these scenes are intended to supply adequate practice material for the average class, without the use of an additional text. Other appendices introduce the beginning student to the director's point of view, as well as to a glossary of stage terms essential to his understanding both of the book and of his work as an actor.

My indebtedness to my teachers and later my colleagues at Cornell University will be everywhere apparent throughout the volume; but I specifically acknowledge it here. Naturally, I share with them a special obligation to James A. Winans. From such standard textbooks as John Dolman's *Art of Play Production* and W. M. Parrish's *Reading Aloud,* which I have used in university classes for a decade or more, I have assimilated much that the trained reader will recognize. Permission to reprint copyright material has been acknowledged at various points throughout the volume.

H. D. A.

ITHACA

Working Up a Part

★★★★★★

1 | Introduction

The scope and the organization of *Working Up A Part* are such as to encourage the inexperienced actor to do as much as possible for himself, in his own way, at his own time, and on his own responsibility. As will be apparent throughout the book, I do not mean to suggest here that dramatic production is at best a patchwork of individualistic interpretations. Dramatic production, on anything above the level of the so-called home talent play and the parlor charade, is a co-operative group activity; and the potentially conflicting ideas of the various performers must be carefully blended with one another in the course of rehearsals. Contemporary theory and practice clearly make the director final judge in such matters, whenever there seem to be differences of opinion or interpretation.

Ideally, however, the actor who is intelligently aware of what is going on, and why, is of considerably more use to the director and the production than the actor who is not; hence the emphasis on individual initiative and responsibility in interpretation. The present volume subscribes to the notion that (unlike the New Deal in election-time stories) the successful student actor knows where he is going when he starts out; he knows how to get there and why; and once he has arrived, he knows where he is. Patterns, motivations, and meanings which have been handed out to him piecemeal and which he has learned blindly and by rote are of little value to his own future development. What is more, they are likely to be of far less value in a given performance than is commonly supposed.

1

It will also soon be apparent to the student that as to *method* or *system* in acting, the book is more or less eclectic — though it inclines toward what is commonly called a natural approach, as opposed to a purely mechanical one. In my view there are too many pitfalls, for the beginner at least, in subscribing without qualification to a single "school" of opinion in this matter. To the inexperienced player, of course, the claims and counter-claims of various systems and procedures may well be merely confusing. He is urged on the one hand to join the "feel-the-emotion" school; on the other, to be an "anti-emotionalist." He is pressed to depend solely on the Russian system, but is then warned to distinguish between Stanislavski, Boleslavsky, Komisarjevsky, and a host of others.

On a somewhat different level, the beginner is urged by some to concern himself chiefly about outer techniques, external manifestations, assumed behaviors, and the like, on the grounds that his inner emotional reaction will then be correct and that in any case he will have called forth a proper emotional response in the audience. At the same time he is urged by others to focus solely on a think-the-thought principle, and to assume that if the "thought" of the playwright has been properly assimilated, proper vocal and bodily expression will automatically follow.

The difficulties arising from an overstrict adherence to either of the last-named systems are well known to experienced players and directors; but it may be well to summarize them here for the student. The devotees of external technique believe that a more or less foolproof system of bodily attitudes and gestures can be set up, by the single means of which emotion and thought can be expressed and projected to an audience. Whether or not the performer "feels" the emotion or "thinks" the thought is irrelevant, since if the external patterns are correct there will be a suitable reaction in the audience. At its best, with a professionally skilled and sensitive performer whose body has been made flexible through long and arduous training, the system is successful. With many actors, the results are stiff, mechanical, unconvincing. At its worst, the system leads to excesses of insincerity and artificiality. Its principal weakness for the amateur lies in the fact that, even if complete mastery of the system were a positive guarantee of successful and convincing performance (which it is not), still the goal of a perfectly and completely trained body which practically alone could carry the burden of emotional expression is much too far in the distance. There is a further weakness for the educational theater, in that too much emphasis is laid on external and mechanical analysis, too little on the development of comprehension and insight in the student.

Advocates of the so-called think-the-thought system believe that if the thought of the character or the playwright is assimilated, perfect vocal and bodily expression will automatically follow. This method has a good deal to recommend it, particularly in educational institutions; but, as its critics sometimes point out, it is apparently a method without a technique. Certainly the untrained student needs more than a simple admonition to focus on the meaning, and then to move and speak as his mind and his feelings will him to do. In the first place, stage reality is an aesthetic, a conventionalized, reality; and there is always an audience to consider. A certain planned exaggeration and heightening of effect are often required to supplement ordinary reactions. Certain external traits of character outside the range of the student-actor's normal behavior may have to be acquired experimentally. Finally, a number of physical or vocal disabilities may come between the inner comprehension and its outward perfect expression.

What actually happens in practice is that the beginning actor uses *both* of these "systems," to the degree and at the time that each serves best. With the guidance and assistance of his director, he creates a visual conception of his character, then imaginatively adapts his voice and body to suit that conception, and ultimately motivates the conception by bringing his real and imagined experience to bear on the character he has thus conceived. No one system, in its extremest form, will serve him at every point in this process.

Two sets of fundamental distinctions in the matter of method may be clarifying for the beginner. The first has already been suggested: what the actor does, and how he does it, *at various stages of study and rehearsal* are in some respects quite different from what he must do *in performance.* While he is building his conception of the character and while he is giving that conception outward form, he needs to experiment — objectively and somewhat mechanically — with various speech and behavior patterns. He needs to observe his own emotional attitudes, as such, and his own movements and gestures, as such. He is forced to test and choose, emphasizing certain external traits but suppressing others. By the later stages of rehearsal, however, the selected patterns of external behavior must have become habitual, so that in performance he can focus with unshakable concentration on the character, the scene, and the point at issue in the dramatic action.

In one of the early rehearsals, an actor may have literally been so moved by the emotional tenseness of a scene that he burst into very real tears. A genuine emotional response of this kind, be it noted, cannot be reproduced night after night; even if it could, the actor could not hold up under the strain, and in any case he would have lost effective control of his body and his mind. Similarly, whole casts have been moved to tears of laughter by the comic aspects of a given scene in rehearsal. Here again actual reproduction of the reaction, with dependable regularity, is neither possible nor desirable. Just how the actor tries to substitute for real emotional reactions symbolic or imagined ones that will serve him in performance is discussed elsewhere in this volume. The point here is that such considerations as "assuming a posture" and "feeling an emotion" are one thing in an experimental rehearsal, quite another in performance.

But there is another — and related — fundamental distinction I would like to emphasize. Too few student-actors distinguish early enough between *vocal and physical freedom and flexibility* on the one hand, and *genuine interpretative skill* on the other. Voice training and body training, *per se*, are not training in *interpretation,* though they free the student of handi-

Liliom and Julie in Ferenc Molnar's LILIOM,
at the Tulane University Theatre.

Flogdell takes a game of checkers, in Samson Raphaelson's
ACCENT ON YOUTH. Iowa State Teachers College Production.

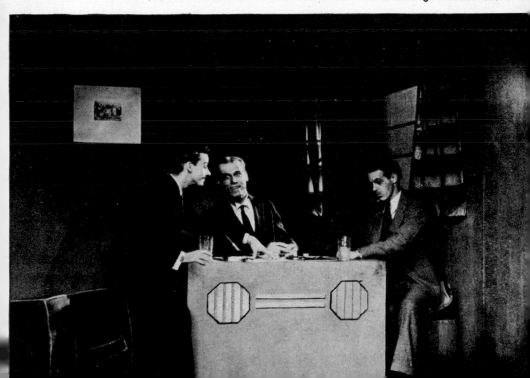

Lucinde and Géronte in Molière's THE DOCTOR IN SPITE
OF HIMSELF. Brooklyn College.

A scene from FAMILY PORTRAIT, by Coffee and Cowen.
William and Mary Theatre.

caps and inhibitions which may at the moment of performance stand in the way of full responsiveness.

Professor Adler, in another connection, has used an analogy that will serve to clarify the distinction. In his *How to Read a Book*,[1] he calls attention to the fact that a prospective tennis player may well have to see a chiropodist if he has corns or blisters on his feet; an oculist if his eyes are weak. He cannot learn the art of tennis unless such handicaps to freedom and flexibility of movement are removed. Even when they are removed, however, as Professor Adler stresses, the individual has still not learned the art of playing tennis. Certain disabilities which prevented him from learning the art have been diagnosed and removed; certain inabilities clearly remain, though he is now at least normally susceptible to training.

That Professor Adler was concerned with "reading" in the sense of grasping meanings from the printed page while we are concerned with oral "reading" as a part of dramatic interpretation is of course irrelevant. The fact remains that no amount of exercise on improving voice quality or range can take the place of understanding and responsiveness at the moment of performance. The understanding and the responsiveness are an integral part of the art of dramatic interpretation. The vocal quality or range is merely a contributing factor, important though it may be. Again, no focus on sounds or on bodily attitudes, as such, can take the place of an actor's concentration on his character and the scene. Indeed, any strong tendency to "think of something else" (e.g., How do I look? How do I sound? What impression or effect am I making?) may result in lost concentration and therefore lost expressiveness.

An actor normally develops in rehearsals a pattern of voice and movement which he can reproduce fairly readily and fairly accurately no matter how little attention he gives to the play. But, as Professor Hewitt has put it,

> ... once his concentration on the character in the play relaxes, the pattern of voice and movement will lose its expressiveness:

1 (Simon & Schuster, 1940), pp. 78-79.

. its learned and automatic character will be revealed. No matter how well lines are learned, they will not be uttered expressively unless they are informed with content by an imagination functioning at the time of utterance. Movement, too, loses its freshness and its expressive power if it is performed merely through kinaesthetic memory and not as the response to inner stimulus, though the mechanical in movement is perhaps less quickly discerned than the mechanical in speech.[2]

These remarks will suffice to indicate the approach to rehearsal and performance which the student is urged to follow, and the method on which he is urged to base his work. If he has had any experience at all, he recognizes that acting and play production are a blend of contributory arts, a unity or conformation that is more than merely a sum of lesser parts. For purposes of study and preparation, however, he must divide his task into workable units; and he must examine each of them separately, if he is to approach rehearsals in a businesslike way. The first of these units, in sequence of time as well as importance, is Analyzing the Part.

[2] Barnard Hewitt, *Art and Craft of Play Production* (Lippincott, 1940), p. 195.

★★★★★★

2 | Analyzing the Part

How can the individual actor set about working up his part? How must he approach his task? Where ought he to begin? He will do best to recognize that he must first examine the *whole* of his play with considerable care. Much of the time he and his fellow-actors are later to spend on rehearsals will be wasted if this preliminary step is slighted in any way. In practice, of course, an early reading is usually held with other actors and the director, so that a relatively uniform general interpretation is agreed upon from the first. In any case — here as elsewhere in the process of play production — a good principle is to start with a whole and to work gradually down to the portions of that whole; to begin with broad meanings and effects, and later to enlarge on these by adding or modifying details.

Your first task as an actor, then, is to consider the play itself as a unit. What, you must ask yourself, does the play mean? What is its purpose? Its basic mood? How, in particular, is it *organized*; what is its structure? If you are like most beginners, you will need to broaden your knowledge as to the nature and scope of dramatic composition.

In characteristic fashion, George Bernard Shaw has defined a play as anything which interests an audience for two hours and a half, on the stage of a theater. His definition has its points; but before you can answer the questions that your job requires you to answer, you will need to probe deeper. As Mr. Shaw has rightly suggested, there are no "rules" or "laws" or "principles" which govern every type of play. The problems that each manuscript raises must be analyzed and solved for themselves. It is possible, however, to outline for you certain

7

basic information that may save valuable time, prevent false steps, and simplify future study.

The Nature of "A Play"

In the first place, then, plays tend to be about *action*, not about words alone. Audiences judge people in plays, as they judge people in life, not so much by what they say as by what they do, by how they respond to other people and to situations. In great and serious plays as well as in very slight ones, written merely to entertain, people are presented in critical or exciting situations; and, in these situations, they reveal themselves by their actions. A good play is not "mostly talk": people move and make decisions, things happen, difficulties are faced and solved. Indeed, the essence of dramatic action is a clash of wills or of wits or of personalities. Some theories of drama [1] hold that a play is normally based on a conflict of opposing forces. The leading character (traditionally called the *protagonist*) has certain ambitions or plans or desires. In these he is opposed by other characters, by social or other forces in the world about him, or by complicating traits within his own nature. The action of the play shows him conquering such opposition, or being conquered or at least frustrated by it; and this conflict is the basis of the dramatic values in the play's presentation. Thus, any production of Howard's *The Silver Cord* would need to focus, in obvious as well as very subtle ways, on the struggle between Christina and Mrs. Phelps. In Odets' *Waiting for Lefty*, the conflict lies clearly between Lefty (and the fellow-workers he represents) and the other "classes"; in O'Neill's *Emperor Jones*, between Jones and his own fears and superstitions.

Other theories, especially more recent ones, hold that *conflict* as used in this connection is too strong a word, and a misleading one with regard to certain types of plays. Among other terms, *crisis* and *dramatic tension* have been put forward

[1] E.g., those of Hegel and Freytag. See Ferdinand Brunetière, *The Law of the Drama* (Dramatic Museum of Columbia University, 1914).

as substitutes more generally applicable; [2] and further attempts have been made to define the nature of "the dramatic." [3] Certainly, in that minority of plays in which conflict is not a strong factor in dramatic development, the student will need to recognize this fact as early as possible and to plan with his director special approaches to his special problems. With most plays, however, and for present purposes, the concept of struggle or conflict is a satisfactory one on which to base one's analysis.

It is through *plot* that the playwright normally makes such a conflict interesting and effective for use on the stage. That is to say, he usually presents a well-organized and closely related series of events, reaching some sort of climax and developing to a more or less logical conclusion. What the playwright has done by way of *wrighting* (in the sense of constructing) his play is of no less significance than what he has done in *writing* it. The chain of events begins with a relatively stable — though potentially UNstable and therefore dramatic — situation. Something then happens to cause a reaction, to upset the *status quo,* and ultimately to bring a new situation. Since the new situation is even more unstable, it leads to a new incident — and therefore to a new reaction and a new state of instability. The sequence of incident-and-situation continues until some kind of decisive action results in a relatively stable situation which "concludes" the play.

As an actor, you will need to examine this sequence of events with painstaking care if you are later to make your portrayal dramatically clear and interesting. Unless you "play the plot" throughout, you will obscure or distort the meaning of the whole; and you will weaken the tension, or suspense, one of the principal means by which the playwright controls the interest of his audience. [4]

[2] The former by William Archer, in *Playmaking* (London, Chapman & Hall, 1912); the latter by Allison Gaw, in "Centers of Interest in Drama, etc.," *Schelling Anniversary Papers* (Century, 1923).

[3] E.g., Allardyce Nicoll, *The Theory of Drama* (London, Harrap, 1931). An excellent brief summary and analysis of various theories appears in Hewitt, *op. cit.,* Part II.

[4] In episodic or other plays with unconventional plot-structure, you must plan with your director other means of maintaining continuity of interest.

Analysis in General

To put it briefly, you will first need to comprehend the *opening situation*, the state of affairs existing at the rising of the curtain. Then, usually quite close to the beginning of the play, comes the *initial incident*, the first event that promises to change or at least to complicate the opening situation. It is the beginning of the dramatic action, the first thing that happens to which the rest of the action may be traced. Nearer the end of the play, on the other hand, is its *climax* — the highest point of interest, the decisive incident toward which all the action has been leading. All events before this climax can in contemporary plays be called rising action, and those which follow it can correspondingly be named falling action.[5] In most short plays and in many long ones, the climax occurs quite near the end of the play; and the falling action, which brings a logical conclusion to the plot's events, is necessarily brief. At this point the conflict has been resolved, the leading character has either won over or lost to his opposition, the audience's suspense as to the outcome has been satisfied, and the play as a whole must end.

In Alice Brown's often-played short comedy, *Joint Owners in Spain,* for example, the opening situation is clearly outlined in the first four pages of dialogue. The curtain rises on a comfortable room in an Old Ladies' Home. Miss Dyer is seen rocking and sighing by a window, ready "at any excuse to dribble into silent tears." Mrs. Fullerton, who has been her roommate, is shakily preparing to leave. A third character, Mrs. Mitchell, a kindly and energetic matron, is hastening the departure. In Mrs. Fullerton's lines and actions, and in the conversation between Mrs. Mitchell and Miss Dyer, the audience comes to

[5] Literary criticism, at least since Freytag, conventionally uses "falling action" in a different sense, as referring to events following a so-called "turning point" near the middle of a play, notably a Shakespearean one. However, I am concerned lest the theater student mistake the traditional concept of falling action (beginning near the middle of a play) for falling *interest*. For the theater student, particularly the beginner, the notion that interest and emotional tension — and therefore action — do not begin to "fall" until the curtain is in sight is a much more useful one.

know Miss Dyer's tearful and complaining ways and her constantly injured air. The spectators are shown her exacting nature, and are informed that so far she has been unable to get along with any of a succession of roommates. They are ready for the initial incident in this dramatic action: the arrival of Mrs. Blair as the latest roommate. They are promised interesting and exciting times, because they already know that Mrs. Blair, too, is notoriously hard to get along with. The ensuing scenes, in which unexpected but satisfying adjustments are made between the two old women, supply rising action. The climax comes on the second-to-the-last page of the manuscript, when Miss Dyer and Mrs. Blair not only agree to go out for a sleigh ride together but insist on helping each other to get ready. The concluding page consists of necessary but falling action. The conflict — between Miss Dyer's will on the one hand, and the opposing forces of both Mrs. Blair and Mrs. Mitchell on the other — has been resolved.

In most plays there are naturally minor climaxes somewhat less decisive in their effect than the main and final one. These must be recognized and played up by the actor no less surely than the principal one. Lack of proper attention to such incidental complications in the plot results in a flat, monotonous, and uninteresting performance. These lesser climaxes often correspond to the crucial points in the incident-and-situation development of the plot, mentioned above. Moreover, the climaxes are often marked by *dramatic reversals,* a playwriting device to which actors and directors must be especially sensitive. The basic situation in any play is likely to be radically altered during the course of the action. One character or group of characters may seem in control of things for a time, but others may gradually gain the upper hand; then, as the play nears its conclusion, the first group (or perhaps still a third) may appear to take control.

In *Joint Owners in Spain,* Miss Dyer was technically in control of the situation at the very beginning of the play, in that she had forced her latest roommate (Mrs. Fullerton) to seek other quarters. Her will-to-control was frustrated, however, by Mrs. Mitchell's decision to bring the equally disagreeable Mrs. Blair to room with her; and on her arrival Mrs. Blair definitely took the upper hand. Later, when Miss Dyer realized the full significance of the chalk marks on the floor, she was tentatively but quite clearly released from the submissive role she had temporarily been forced to play in her own room. And finally, she was wholly free once more to take a superior position in the household when, near the end of the play, she could play grand hostess to the matron and airily invite Mrs. Blair to "come right through her house and save a step." These reversals help to divide the play into several clearly defined units or scenes. If the reversals themselves were not marked by the actors, or if the several units in the action were not contrasted one with the other, the final performance would be noticeably weakened.

What I have here called scenes or units of action must therefore be recognized and fixed in the actor's mind early in the course of his analysis. The limits of such scenes [6] (sometimes named "structural scenes" or "rehearsal scenes") may or may not correspond exactly to each new entrance or exit of the various characters in the play, as in the French drama. It is a more useful practice to conceive of the limits of structural scenes as marked by the entrance or exit of *major* characters, or of *major groups* or *series* of characters. The observant student will find that such entrances and exits usually mark the beginning and ending of workable dramatic units. He will note that each unit tends to have a structural development of its own, with a beginning, middle, and end. Each has a discernible purpose, tone, style, meaning, and over-all function of its own, especially as compared with others in the same act or play. Some actors and directors go so far as to give each structural scene a carefully phrased title or theme, as a means of infusing it with special purpose and meaning.

A workable scheme for rehearsal scenes in Act I of Raphael-

---

[6] They are not to be confused, of course, with "scenes" of other established connotations (e.g., scenes as places of action; as settings; as divisions of a play which, while shorter than an act, do run from curtain to curtain).

son's *Accent on Youth,* for example, might run as follows: Scene i (about five pages in the acting version), between Linda and the actors; ii (about five pages), between Steven and the actors; iii (three pages), Steven and Linda; iv (nine pages), Steven and Genevieve; v (one page), Steven and Flogdell; and vi (eleven pages), Steven and Linda.[7] Since, as has been stressed in the preceding paragraph, these six scenes will be found to vary widely in nature and purpose, an actor who appeared in any of them would have to take precautions to insure that each scene maintained its own individual characteristics during performance. Naturally enough, the actor's chief interest is the scene or scenes in which he himself appears; but he must be aware throughout of his own scene's place in the dramatic development, and of its relation to other scenes.

On the other hand, the beginner should be warned that, despite such individualization of the several scenes, the unifying mood or spirit of the whole must never be seriously violated. Each scene is a contributing unit in a larger pattern; each must blend with its neighbors in a consistent general effect. In comedy, for example, no matter how "serious" affairs may be at the moment, a generally optimistic tone must prevail; to suggest any other would be merely to confuse or mislead the audience. As a part of his analysis, therefore, the actor must decide what the prevailing mood of his play should be, and how his own role and his own scenes should fit into the general scheme. The play may be fundamentally serious, even tragic. It may be mockingly satiric, gently humorous, broadly comic. It may of course be a composite of several of these, or of others; but its dominant mood must be recognized as early as possible.

The traditional analysis of plays by literary types — tragedy, serious drama, comedy-drama, melodrama, comedy, and farce

---

[7] Note that the brief entrance of Flogdell on page 22 of the script has not been treated as a separate dramatic unit. While this is no ordinary "butler's announcement" (Flogdell is no ordinary butler!), yet it has not the length, scope, or point to demand separate consideration; it does have special function as part of one of the larger units. Compare the treatment of Flogdell's second entrance, Scene v, above.

— is naturally of importance to the actor, and he should be familiar with standard dramatic criticism.[8] Tragedy and comedy are usually treated as basic types, with the others as intermediate types or as extreme modifications of the basic ones. The student should recognize that in general the material of tragedy may well be similar to that of comedy. The significant difference lies in the playwright's attitude toward his material and in his treatment of it. The actor and director must differentiate, over a wide range of mood and attitude, on the basis of the emotional reaction intended in the audience. That a character suffers, for example, is in itself no indication of how an audience is to *take* the suffering; clearly, the suffering may be acted as a serious consequence of human weakness or stupidity, or may be treated lightly, even farcically, in a spirit of laughter and play.

Such matters as mood are in some respects chiefly the concern of your director, who is the "designer" of your production; but he will welcome your interest and your understanding from the beginning. The same is true of what may be called the aesthetic style of your production. The director will help you recognize and project certain marked differences between such so-called presentational plays as Wilder's *Happy Journey* or *Our Town* and such so-called representational ones as most of Ibsen's or Chekhov's. If your play is Rice's *Adding Machine* or its continental predecessor, Kaiser's *Morn to Midnight,* he will introduce you to expressionistic theory and practice. If, on the other hand, your play is fantastic rather than realistic in style, your director will help you master the special difficulties involved. Detailed distinctions of the sort broadly indicated here are somewhat beyond the scope of this handbook, but they will have to make up still another part of your analysis; some elementary suggestions are offered in Appendix B.

---

[8] The types listed above are defined and briefly discussed in Part I of Appendix D. For more detailed treatment, see Hewitt, *op. cit.*; Milton Marx, *The Enjoyment of Drama* (Crofts, 1940); and Nicoll, *op. cit.* See also Barrett H. Clark, *European Theories of the Drama,* rev. ed. (Crown, 1947). Further readings on dramatic theory in general, as well as on the tragic and the comic, are listed in Part II of Appendix D in the present volume.

Finally, you will have to include in your analysis some consideration of the play's *point* — its over-all and unifying meaning. The title may be instructive, as in *The Silver Cord, A Doll's House,* and *The Circle.* The playwright may have furnished a significant quotation, possibly printed on the title page, which will serve as a clue. Or one of the key speeches of a central character may be an explicit statement of the theme. Various of these devices may be combined, as in the "Take us the foxes, the little foxes that spoil the vines" of Lillian Hellman's play. Of course, the basic idea of the play may be implicit in the text, rather than explicit, in which case the actors should strive to encompass the meaning in as specific a statement as seems possible to attain. In some plays a theme, as such, is not strongly stressed by the playwright; but this does not necessarily mean that no theme is there, and failure to discover and project it would be a vital failure indeed. I have, I must admit, seen amateur players so obsessed with "theme" that they played light comedies as serious problem dramas. But that is another matter.

It is best not to look upon finding the theme as a mere exercise in intellectual gymnastics. In some cases you may not wish to call the process "finding a theme" at all, and you may not be able or willing to force your idea about the play into the specific statement required in the preceding paragraph. In other cases, you may wish to identify or combine the process with a search for the author's purpose in writing the play, or the author's life-attitude or world-attitude as he has expressed it in this play and possibly in others. You may prefer, as some people do, to call what you are looking for the play's "core" or "*leit-motif*" or "Idea." But — with your director, of course — you usually cannot avoid some decision as to *what the play is fundamentally about,* as to what essential and unique characteristics set it apart from other plays of broadly similar plots and situations.

The Part in Relation to the Play

When the prospective actor has become familiar with the structure of his play, and when he has to some degree clarified in his own mind the play's meaning, style, and spirit, he is ready to consider his particular functions in the whole. These functions — in the play as a unit as well as in individual scenes — must always be one of the principal guides to the player's behavior.

Careful examination will usually show that most characters are ranged on one side or the other of the play's basic conflict. You may find that your character is one of a group supporting the ambition or desire of the protagonist; or, conversely, one of a group opposing it. Your particular character may have decided to support the protagonist as a friend, relative, or adviser. He may be called upon to support the protagonist as an employee. Or, in similar ways and for similar reasons, your character may be drawn up on the opposite side of the conflict. On the other hand, you may be playing one of several minor parts introduced by the author to echo or reinforce the basic conflict in terms of a subordinate but similar one. Perhaps the subordinate situation is meant to offer contrast to, rather than reinforcement for, the main conflict.

The part you are to play may not directly support any of the two or more conflicting groups. In this case, it may be introduced principally for exposition — for telling important information necessary to the audience's understanding of the action, but not clearly presented elsewhere. Or the purpose of your part may be chiefly to furnish background, local color, or atmosphere. As such, it would help to clarify the opening situation, or some unit in the rising action, or both. Naturally, the purpose may vary from scene to scene, with emphasis centered in sequence on exposition, characterization, atmosphere, plot, and idea, or on some blending of several of these.

It should be obvious that quite small parts can often be tremendously *important* parts, and that the value and significance of a role does not depend merely on its "size." Taking *Joint*

Owners in Spain as an example once more, note that Mrs. Fullerton's relatively short part at the beginning of the play is vital in outlining the opening situation. Except for her living presence, the existing state of affairs could only be talked about; and the later action of the play would consequently be neither so clear nor so interesting as it now turns out to be. As a matter of fact, if the part of Mrs. Fullerton is at all well played, audiences tend to remember her vividly and to recognize her pointed contribution to the total effect. Much the same could be said of Mrs. Mitchell. Technically, she is certainly not the leading character in the play. Yet without her contributions to the exposition in the opening scene and without her firm opposition to Miss Dyer at several points in the action, the play would be dull and extremely hard to follow. Furthermore, her relative disinterestedness in the personal bickerings of the inmates affords dramatic contrast throughout, and her natural authority as a person and as the matron lends balance and continuity to the play.

Several dramatic functions are, of course, occasionally combined in a single character or group of characters, but this need not be confusing. The important point to bear in mind is that every actor must be both clear and definite about his essential purpose in a play before he can make the most of the rehearsal periods.

The Part in Itself

By this time certain more or less specific questions may well have occurred to you. What, for instance, ought your character to *look* like? How ought he to move? Is he heavy, strong, forceful; or is he habitually weak and indecisive? Under ordinary circumstances, would he stand erect and at ease, or would he tend to slouch? Would his posture usually suggest stiffness, awkwardness; informality, assurance? Would he stride or pace? Mince; plod; shuffle? How would his general, day-by-day appearance be modified by the special requirements of the situations in the play? In his bodily attitudes or movements could an observer note definite signs of his age? His occupation? His nationality? His state of health?

You will not be able to answer such questions, and others that may arise, after merely one or two readings of the play. You can answer them fully and satisfactorily only after you have known your character for some time, and have learned *why* he says the things he says, believes the things he believes, and does the things he does.[9] But you will need to start at the very beginning to formulate a set of rather definite ideas about his habits and appearance. You will naturally want to modify these ideas as you go along; to change them, add to them, and clarify them. Nevertheless, you cannot begin too early to visualize the general impression that your character gives as he walks, stands, sits, or gestures.

You had better begin early, also, to consider how he *sounds*. Is his voice habitually coarse or smooth or metallic? Heavy or light? Is he noisy in his movements? Does he ordinarily slam doors, scrape chairs, toss books loudly on the table; or is it natural for him to be careful and quiet about such simple daily actions? How would his customary habits in these respects be influenced by the basic situation in the play, or by the special situation in certain scenes? Your ability to answer these questions, too, will grow with your intimate acquaintance with the personality of the character you are studying. In the meantime, try to be aware of such problems as you move along.

You can further enrich your understanding of your character if you now think about him in a slightly different way. How, you might ask yourself, is he like other persons in the play? How is he like other persons you know? On the other hand — and this is perhaps more important — how is he *different*? What makes him unique, gives him his individuality? What is it that sets him off, in more or less dramatic contrast, from the other characters in the action?

One of the weakest features in many amateur productions is that all the actors seem to move and talk alike, and to react

[9] In this connection, see the chapter on characterization, especially pages 81-85.

in the same way to people and situations. Necessary differences in age, status, and personality are glossed over. The result is often dullness and monotony; or, what is in some ways worse, lack of clarity. Individual characterizations and reactions must always be clearly differentiated. Otherwise major and minor conflicts are hidden, reversals and other contrasts underplayed, and dramatic effects in general minimized. Naturally, it should be easy for the audience to spot differences, contrasts, and changes on the stage; certainly it should be in no sense difficult, as it will be if characters are not individualized.

Finding the Answers to Your Questions

But where are you to look for the answers to the questions you have asked yourself thus far? On what will you base your replies? What facts have you at hand to stimulate your ingenuity and your imagination? The basic source of your information, quite evidently, must be the play itself. The mainsprings of your character's personality and actions, the cues for both speech and movement, will always be suggested in the author's manuscript. Such details will frequently be difficult to find, but the fact is that they will usually be there.

One of the more obvious sources in the play book is the author's preliminary description of his characters, either in his listing of the cast or at the time of each character's first entrance. But there are other less obvious, though at the same time more fruitful, sources of information. For instance, there may be descriptions of your character's appearance, personality, or habits scattered through the speeches of other characters. None of these descriptions may be overlooked, whether it is explicitly stated or merely suggested. And quite apart from their lines, the other characters may imply by their actions what certain traits in your own character must be. One of the others might clearly suggest, for example, either by lines or by action, that your character is always late, or that he usually talks too much, or that he can regularly be depended upon in time of trouble. The author may never have written these tendencies out for you in so many words, yet they would necessarily be important aspects of your character's personality and even of his appearance.

The author has usually introduced other hints for your characterization. The stage directions he has written into your part are in themselves a fertile source of suggestion. For example, does he usually write that you respond eagerly and promptly; or does he indicate that you are diffident or slow or lazy? Does he have you take a firm stand on things, or are you meant to be vague, uncertain, weak? Does he suggest, directly or indirectly, just how you might normally move, speak, or react? Are there certain scenes in which the patterns he suggests are quite the opposite? The possibilities here, especially if your separate stage directions are considered in relation to one another, are almost unlimited. In studying as well as in rehearsing your part, be sure to concentrate on the stage directions; never "take them for granted."

Above all, critically examine your own speeches. In any well-written play, these are, after all, the primary sources of information about the character you are to portray. What your character threatens directly to do or not to do, to believe or not to believe, ought usually to be your best cue for motivation and for action. Even if at some points he does not mean what he says, this fact in itself will suggest certain traits that you must bring out in your total characterization. You must always be careful, of course, to look below the surface of your lines. In some scenes, characters may either deliberately or unconsciously cover up their true intentions; and if you allow yourself to be misled by these scenes, you will certainly end up by misleading the audience.

Further suggestions on characterization will be reserved for a later chapter. As I have already indicated, character-building is a slow process, moving gradually from the general to the particular, and extending from the earliest reading of the manuscript to the last rehearsal before performance. The important point at the moment is that the sharper and the clearer you can make the *broad outlines* of your characterization during the first weeks of the process, the better chances you will ultimately have of doing an interesting and effective job.

Your analysis may seem to have absorbed a good deal of your time and to have taken you far afield, though time wisely used at this point is time saved severalfold later on. Adequate understanding of a role and of its functions in a play may not guarantee adequate performance. For most players, however, adequate performance is unlikely *without* the understanding, and the understanding had better come first.

To help bring your ideas into focus, a check-list of questions on the content of the present chapter is given below. Similar lists will follow other chapters in the volume; taken together, these lists will suggest to you a workable plan of procedure in preparing future roles. Remember that: (1) your answers should be specific; and (2) they ought to be in keeping with the over-all design of your director.

CHECK–LIST ON ANALYSIS

1. What is the meaning of your play as a whole? Can you briefly but clearly describe its style? Its prevailing mood?
2. Where is the initial incident in the plot? The climax? What separate incidents or situations make up the rising action? Where are the minor climaxes? The reversals?
3. Have you properly divided the action into *scenes*, for study and rehearsal? Can you describe the nature and purpose of each?
4. What is the play's basic conflict? Are there subordinate conflicts? Do these (a) echo or (b) contrast with the main one?
5. Is your character ranged on the side of the main character? On the opposite side? On neither?
6. Has your character been introduced chiefly for exposition, local color, or atmosphere? For some combination of reasons?
7. What, in general, does your character look like? How does he sound? How does he react to people and to situations?
8. How is he like other persons in the play; other persons you know? How is he different?

9. As an actor, what can you learn about your character from the play book? In your own stage directions? In your own lines, from what is said or implied as well as from what is denied or misrepresented? In the lines or actions of the other characters?

EXERCISES FOR CHAPTER 2

I. (a) Write out, as a declarative statement, the theme of such short plays as *The (Marriage) Proposal, The Flattering Word, Wurzel-Flummery,* and *Riders to the Sea.*[10] To what degree is idea, *per se,* strongly evident in each play; and to what degree must the idea in each be stressed and projected in performance?

(b) How is the relative importance of the theme in each influenced by — and what is its influence on — the prevailing mood or the style? What might be the result of overstressing the theme in such a play as *Wurzel-Flummery,* at the expense of characterization, atmosphere, or plot?

(c) Compare Ibsen's *A Doll's House* with his *Hedda Gabler,* with respect to focus on the theme, as such.

(d) How would you describe the prevailing mood of *Claudia? Winterset? The Front Page? The Little Foxes? Escape? Our Town? The Petrified Forest? Private Lives? Dear Brutus?*

II. (a) A plan of structural or rehearsal scenes for Act I of *Accent on Youth* appears on page 13 of this chapter. Draw up a plan for Act II.

(b) Where are the (minor) climaxes in Acts I and II? The reversals?

(c) Mark the limits of satisfactory rehearsal scenes for other long and short plays, such as *Liliom, The Silver Cord,* or *Candida; Spreading the News, Minnie Field,* or *The Boor.* Comment on the nature and function of the several scenes.

III. (a) Indicate the basic conflict in *Hedda Gabler;* in *Rocket to the Moon;* in *Hamlet.*

---

[10] All of these plays appear in Helen Louise Cohen, *One-Act Plays,* rev. ed. (Harcourt, Brace, 1938); but similar plays from another collection would serve as well. With few exceptions, the plays used as examples in the text and in the exercises have been published in one or more collections as well as in an acting version. A number of the plays mentioned appear in abbreviated form in the "The Best Plays" series, edited by Burns Mantle (Dodd, Mead, 1920 to date).

(*b*) Can you cite plays in which the element of conflict is not so important, or at least so obvious? How, without the normal suspense of developing conflict, do these plays hold the interest of an audience?

IV. (*a*) Choose a character, other than the protagonist, from one of the plays already mentioned in these exercises — e.g., Mr. Prince in *Rocket to the Moon*; Garth in *Winterset*; Frank Galloway in *Accent on Youth*. Describe the dramatic function of the part, and the character's relation to the basic conflict.

(*b*) In *Accent on Youth*, what is the purpose of the author's introduction of the Galloway and Flogdell marriages? In *Winterset*, note Miriamne's divided loyalties with respect to taking sides in the basic conflict. In *Rocket to the Moon*, comment on Cleo's development, as a character and as a person, throughout the play.

(*c*) Choose other characters from similar plays, and analyze them in the manner suggested above.

V. (*a*) For two characters in one of the plays you have already chosen, write out in detail answers to Questions 7 and 8 in the *Check-list on Analysis*.

(*b*) For one of these characters, answer the various parts of Question 9 in the *Check-list*; cite specific pages and lines in support of your replies.

VI. Compare Cleopatra in Shakespeare with Cleopatra in Shaw; Electra in Euripides with Electra in von Hofmannsthal; a lover, hero, cynic, or scoundrel in a contemporary play of your choice with a similar character in another play. How might your approach to the playing of the same character (or the same general type of character) in the several plays be affected by differences in form, style, or theme within the plays themselves?

VII. Repeat Exercises V and VI, above, after you have studied the chapter on characterization.

3 | Rehearsing the Part: Movement

The actor's analysis, if it is as far-reaching as the previous chapter has recommended, can start him on his way toward mastery of his role. It can help him to sense the direction which his interpretation must ultimately take. It can make him aware of the problems of movement and gesture, voice and speech, which the part will entail. Finally, it can lay the foundations for the first main step in character-building: *creating a conception* of his character.

As a further step in the same process, the actor must now give outward form and substance to his conception. Having created a mental image, he must imaginatively adapt his voice and his body to suit that image. He must begin to suppress personal traits that would be foreign to his role. Under the guidance of his director, he must assume in rehearsal patterns of movement and of speech that will set his character apart from the others, and that will clarify the intellectual and emotional meanings which the playwright intended. As he assumes these patterns of behavior, moreover, he must bear in mind constantly that the playwright's meanings must ultimately be projected from a stage, to an audience, in a theater.

Although in some respects "a character is indivisible," yet the actor's voice and the actor's bodily movement do make distinct contributions to a total characterization, and both offer specialized problems for the beginner. For purposes of study and rehearsal, therefore, each will be given separate treatment; and movement will be considered first.

The Basic Importance of Movement and Gesture

The importance of pantomime — i.e., the expression of dramatic ideas through movement and gesture alone — is often underestimated by the beginning actor. When his portions of the play's dialogue have been memorized, he is likely to feel that his major task has been accomplished. Actually, he has a double task: first, to learn his *part,* rather than merely the lines; and second, to communicate that part to his audience. And in the process of such communication, the separate speeches of the actors are but one means of expression; pantomime is another, of at least equal importance.

As a matter of fact, most people express themselves in bodily reactions and attitudes before they do in speech. They reveal themselves first by their movements, by their mannerisms of face or of body. They express themselves by what they do or refrain from doing. And only then, as a general rule, do they add vocally their more detailed reactions. In normal situations, for example, people lean toward an object or a person that interests them; they turn away when they are disgusted or have lost interest; they become visibly tense when they are worried or frightened. They slump in their chairs, straighten their shoulders, shake their heads, or brace themselves for a shock, depending on what is going on in their minds. They suggest in their whole bodily attitudes their joy, their anger, their embarrassment, their indecision, or their despair. That is to say, they *communicate* directly with anyone who is watching; and, in a general way, the watcher knows what they are thinking and what they are likely to do.

If this is true in real life, it is all the more so on the stage. The spectator cannot guess what you as an actor are thinking and feeling: he must have some outward indication of your intentions; he knows only what he sees and hears. If he merely hears an important dramatic idea, but never "sees" it, his impression is so much the weaker. Moreover, he must get his impressions from a distance. As Professor Drummond has put it,[1] the spectator cannot read your palm or feel your pulse; he must learn what you are and what you mean by your posture or your carriage.

The expressive value of properly assumed bodily attitudes can be put in still another way. According to some schools of psychology as well as some schools of acting, an inner emotional state is not merely the cause of outward bodily attitudes; it is at least partially the result of them. That is to say, an outward imitation of attitudes suggesting suffering, for example, will help to bring the corresponding inner feelings. Repeated physical outbursts suggesting anger will definitely increase an inner urge to extreme passion. If one feeds a melancholy by dismal posturings and sighings, the melancholy deepens, but if he deliberately assumes a brighter and more cheerful aspect and posture, the melancholy tends to disappear.

Psychologists are in dispute as to the exact cause-and-effect relationship involved here, though they would tend to agree that inner states of mind and outer physical attitudes do exert a general influence on each other, and that this influence is demonstrable. Indeed, you can test for yourself the validity of such a theory. If you have difficulty seeming natural and convincing in your vocal expression of anger, fear, or remorse, assume the proper bodily attitude and observe the result. You will certainly find it easier to be expressive vocally; and you may find that you have enlarged your expressive possibilities generally. Conversely, you will find it difficult, if not impossible, to express your inner feelings effectively if your posture and movement deny or misrepresent that state. By way of example, try to communicate fury while sulkily slumping in an easychair; or to communicate depression and despair while standing firmly and erectly, chest out, head up. In stage rehearsals as in life, appropriate action tends to produce the de-

---

[1] In: A. M. Drummond, *A Manual of Play Production* (Ithaca, New York, published by the author, 1930). This is a concise exposition of sound and practical rules for both actor and director; a reprint of *Play Production for the Country Theatre* (1924), it has had wide use for many years.

sired mood. Tense, quick, restless movement not only appears agitated, but tends to produce agitation; relaxed ease on an overstuffed sofa not only appears calm, but tends to be calm.

Pantomimic action, then, is (1) usually preliminary to speech, and (2) always fundamental to expression. As has already been implied in Chapter 2, such action is also the true basis of characterization. An actor can rarely communicate his station in life, his age, his habits of mind, or his emotional nature by his voice alone. His movement and posture are his calling card. They tell who he is, where he has been, and what he represents; and they speak quickly, clearly, and directly.

The Actor's Physical Requirements

To insure the most effective bodily communication, an actor requires a healthy and flexible body. Dancing and certain forms of athletics (e.g., swimming, boxing, gymnastics, and especially fencing) have traditionally been recommended as suitable means of physical development for the prospective actor. Such activities subordinate the part to the whole, and focus on smooth and balanced functioning of the body as a complex but single organism. Isolated exercises which tend to develop muscle-systems or parts of the body separately and without regard to their function in the whole, have usually proved less satisfactory. Individual exercises to develop poise, balance, and co-ordination are of course another matter.

It would be misleading to imply that only athletes or dancers can successfully perform a typical play. But the chances for an adequate performance are clearly dependent on an actor's physical *vitality,* his physical *control,* and his physical *responsiveness.* The only good actor is an alert actor. The player who is physically ill or weary, or just not concentrating both body and mind on the tasks at hand, is in difficulty before he starts. Prompt and vivid responses, important as they are to the clarity and interest of a scene, are simply beyond the reach of an actor who is not "on his toes." A body only half alive at the moment of rehearsal or performance is a body more than half useless to the director. Even the shortest scene demands warmth and vitality and genuine concentration from every actor concerned.

But beyond such vitality, every scene demands physical *control.* Alertness or energy that is not disciplined is likely to be distracting as well as meaningless on the stage. Any movement that is clearly visible to the spectators has a strong claim on their attention. Hence the actor must move only when his part and the scene require that he move, and never otherwise. This is apparently one of the most difficult lessons for the beginner to learn, yet it is one of the most important. If a gesture or movement is not going to contribute to the dramatic meaning of a scene — or to draw attention to something that is contributing such meaning — then that action is either unnecessary or misleading, or both. Rapidly and absent-mindedly moving the hands from hips to pockets and back again; nodding the head on almost every phrase; shifting the weight constantly back and forth from foot to foot; sidestepping or otherwise shifting about while others are speaking — each of these is monotonous and distracting. Each may be a carryover from real-life habits, or a result of nervous tensions of the moment. But each is fatal to expressive communication.

When the actor does move or gesture, he must do so freely but economically. A performer who is physically tense calls attention to himself rather than to the character or the scene. Alertness and vitality must not be taken to imply taut nerves and stiffened muscles. Teachers of acting of markedly different backgrounds and temperaments unite in counseling their students to relax. Expressive movement, as well as efficient voice production, require freedom from undue strain and tension. Like the dancer and the singer, every actor must learn to use those muscles which are directly concerned with the business at hand, and to let the others alone. Effective movements on the stage must usually seem effortless, though of course they must rarely seem weak.

An actor's *responsiveness* is his third physical requirement. He must seem, at the moment of performance, to be *in con-*

tact with the people and the things about him. He must listen, react, and reply; he must touch, react, and draw back; he must see, react, and respond. Whatever his cue for moving or speaking, he must adjust himself to what has been seen, heard, felt, smelled, or tasted; and must then effectively "answer back." He must show that he has received an impression. He must not only think, but feel, his way about.

Most beginners are noticeably weak in this respect. They move about a room as though they were sleep-walking: they do not appear to see the doors, the furniture, or the other persons on the stage. They handle a heavy object as though it were light as a feather, carry a book as though it were a box of high explosives, use a telephone as though it were something they did not recall having seen before. An actress, playing a housewife, performs as though the well-worn furniture in her own living room were new and strange, touches it or sits down in it as though it belonged to somebody else. An actor seems to recognize newly arrived visitors before he has really had time to see or to hear them. Others appear dumbfounded by events seconds before such events could possibly have registered on their consciousness.

And so it goes from scene to scene. The performer's lack of awareness of his surroundings, of reaction to his cues, continually mars the convincingness of his work.[2] The spectators may not be sure just what is wrong; they may only have some vague feeling that the scene is not going well. But as long as the actors' "contact" is weak, the spectators' interest will be correspondingly weak, and the scene will lack clarity and conviction.

Efficiency in Posture and Movement

Before the student is ready to move easily about on the stage, and before he is ready to assume the individualized

[2] The beginner should note that full freedom to react to surroundings depends on an early memorization of his director's plan for his key positions and movements.

patterns of behavior which his role will ultimately demand, he must be clear about what is "normal" or "natural" in posture and movement. It would be unscientific (as well as valueless for the actor) to hold up a single inflexible standard for all persons under all circumstances, yet it is possible to make certain generalizations that are both valid and useful. Normal and natural posture for the actor, most teachers agree, must mean efficient posture. Neither as stiff as the proverbial ramrod nor as limp as the proverbial gunnysack, the actor must be alert, alive, ready to react on stimulus. "Good" posture for the actor is not fixed or stable, but dynamic; the body is adjusted to the needs of the existing situation and is prepared to move or react with a minimum expenditure of effort.

Normally, the standing body should be straight. The actor's head should be directly above the chest, hips, and feet; the chest should be held relatively high and forward, the abdomen relatively firm and flat; the usual curves of the back should not be exaggerated. The weight should be in easy balance. If the weight is shifted primarily to one foot, it should not be over-shifted; there must be no exaggerated side bend at the hips. The actor who slumps on the weight-bearing side is not only unpleasant to look at, but is unprepared to move as the action may dictate.

The walking body is normally poised, balanced. An ungainly and therefore distracting walk is usually due to jerky or awkward shifts of body weight. In general, the torso is upright and moves directly forward, without swaying from side to side, bending backward and forward, or bouncing up and down on every other step. There should be no impression of weakness or slovenliness. On the other hand there should be no impression of pomposity or swagger, as though the actor as a person were trying to compensate for embarrassment or a sense of inferiority.

In normal sitting positions, the hips should be pushed far enough back in relation to the upper body that the natural curve of the spine can be generally maintained. If the torso slumps so that the spine is thrown into a long single curve, then the chest cannot poise easily above the hips and the abdominal muscles and organs are subjected to undue strain and pressure. Sprawling and slouching are of course to be avoided, as is exaggerated stiffness or rigidity. Just as with standing and walking, a sense of easy and "ready" poise is the ideal.

The student should note that the normal, uncharacterized behavior here described offers distinct advantages to the actor. Such behavior allows full freedom for efficient and clear-cut action that is without irrelevant distractions for the audience. Moreover, the behavior suggested is of major importance to proper breathing, a function which is to be discussed in a succeeding chapter. Finally, it frees the actor — that is to say, as an individual — of special personal traits or attitudes of his own which might have misleading dramatic significance. Until he has rid himself of outstanding habits of behavior strongly at variance with the normal, he is not prepared to assume the particularized traits of his character.

General Principles for Stage Movement

It may be useful at this point to suggest several general principles on which an actor's action-patterns may be based. The first of these has already been implied: *Move only for a specific dramatic purpose.* Random movements of the hands, the feet, or the head must be either suppressed entirely or adapted to fit some purposeful action. Unless as an actor you see and understand a definite reason for moving from place to place on the stage, do nothing at all. To this charge your director can allow no exception.

When you do move, on the other hand, your movement ought to contribute unmistakably either to the meaning of your own part or to the meaning of the scene as a whole. A few examples will serve to establish the point. You may have to move toward a window because the plot requires that you are later to see someone approaching. You may need to move about in a certain way to indicate your character's personality or his present state of mind; or perhaps to emphasize an important point in the dialogue. You may need to move to show a change. If you wished to make clear that you had no intention of prolonging an argument, you might turn or even move away; and, conversely, turning back and moving closer to your opponent would suggest that you intended to begin in earnest.

Your purposeful movements, on the other hand, may serve to direct attention to another actor who has something significant to do or to say at the moment. You might accomplish this result by looking toward him, by seeming to listen carefully, or merely by getting out of his way so that the audience can better see his action. In this connection, note that one of the actor's primary functions in interpreting a play is to control the attention of his audience. The spectator should look where the actor wants him to look, and listen to what the actor wants him to listen to, *when* the actor wishes.[3] If the spectator's attention is dispersed, or if he is looking at or listening to the wrong things, he may lose track of the main trends of the action.

This fact leads to a second major principle: *Make your movements clear, firm, and deliberate.* Half a gesture is often worse than none. An uncertain or indeterminate movement usually carries the false suggestion of timidity or weakness, and it may fail to catch and properly lead the audience's attention. When you turn to look at another character, for example, ordinarily turn most of the way, and make the turn clearly evident with the body as well as the head. Lead, so to speak, with the eyes; then follow with the head, the torso, and the legs. Be especially careful to avoid the predicament of seeming to have your feet glued to the floor, facing out, while your head, arms, and torso are twisted awkwardly in some other direction. Similarly, do not allow one part of your body to remain relaxed and unexpressive while another does its best to carry meaning. In general, "follow through" on a movement, if you wish to be both clear and natural.

[3] For further discussion of controlled attention, as it concerns both actor and director, see Appendix A, pages 113-117.

Another aspect of clarity in movement depends on doing one thing at a time. This implies, first of all, that you strip your pantomime of unnecessary minor movements and gestures. Select only those bits of movement which are absolutely necessary to suggest the action required, and rigorously exclude all others. Thus you will bring a single significant action clearly into focus for the audience.

Should the action naturally contain two or three separate parts, be sure not to muddle them together or try to do all of them at once. Let us assume that you are seated stage right, and that you are to exit angrily and excitedly on the cue of another actor's line. The stage directions in the author's manuscript may merely indicate: "He sputters and rushes out in anger." Assuredly, you must hear the speech first and give it time to register. Only then can you gasp or sputter as the situation may require; rise and glare at the speaker; and finally hurry off the stage in characteristic fashion. Only if these separate moves are not jumbled together can they add clarity, naturalness, and indeed climax to the scene. Your job is to make a point of each single impression, be sure it has registered, and then proceed to the next.

The best formula for any sustained bit of pantomime is to (a) "think" the action, (b) "see" the action, and only then (c) "do" the action — and do it clearly and deliberately. If an important scene requires that you drink medicine, for instance, first see and feel the glass and the bottle; carefully pour the medicine from the bottle, and deliberately watch it run into the glass; then drink it naturally and set the properties down firmly. Suppress every unnecessary motion, but do not hurry those that remain.

A third general principle, which grows out of the others, is quickly stated: *Don't overdo.* Exaggerated facial expressions, artificial gestures, mechanical postures detract rather than add to the interest and meaning of a typical scene. When in doubt, do less rather than more; be restrained rather than violent. Above all, control your physical expression "from the inside." Stay in character, but except for purposeful movement, keep still. Such behavior not only gives the other characters and the scene itself a chance to register on the minds of the audience; but it also serves to emphasize your own movements when you finally do make them.

In connection with these principles of movement, a final suggestion may prove valuable. Once you have — with your director — set your pattern of movement for the entire play, it is well to walk through that pattern from time to time, without lines, but with careful attention to positions, postures, and necessary bits of action. This will serve to polish your movement and to keep it connected, smooth, and natural. If you have your director or some other interested person observe your pantomime on such an occasion, it may also serve to check on the contributions which your body, your carriage, and your gestures are making toward a complete characterization.

★ ★ ★   *Some Practical Rules-of-Thumb*   ★ ★ ★

Move about the stage in relatively straight lines; use the shortest path from point to point. This makes for economy and precision. Shallow curves may of course be required from time to time, as when furniture or other actors bar the most direct path. Wide curves, however, usually suggest weakness or uncertainty, or preoccupation with the movement *per se*; and wide curves usually consume too much time.

In moving from one part of the stage to another, step out with the foot nearest the point to which you are going. The general effect of tangled legs and feet that results from failure to observe this rule is decidedly awkward on the stage. If you maintain a balanced normal posture, you will not be caught off guard but will always be ready to shift your weight unobtrusively from one leg to the other so that you can readily start out with the proper foot.

Stand and sit with the foot that is away from the audience advanced slightly; usually give the audience a three-quarters view of your face; if you are turning your body from right to left, or vice versa, usually turn facing the audience. Be sure you are justified before breaking this rule, though do not hesitate to break it when necessary. On the whole, play the play toward the audience.

Come well onstage as you enter; don't linger in the entrance. Contrariwise, try to speak the last few words or lines of a scene from somewhere near the exit. If you finish speaking too far from the exit, and the other actors withhold their speeches — as they usually must — until you are gone, there will be an awkward and undramatic pause.

Try to play most of the important scenes relatively downstage (i.e., near the audience). On the whole, your visual and auditory effectiveness weakens as you play farther away from the audience. On the other hand, never wander so far downstage as to seem "out of the scene."

Learn to compensate for other characters' necessary movements by readjusting your own position in relation to the group. "Dress the stage" whenever possible; don't be overly formal about it, but keep the grouping in balance unless some other arrangement is clearly indicated.

Make important crosses downstage of the furniture and of the other actors; in this way you will rightly focus audience attention on your movement. Crosses that are meant to pass relatively unnoticed should be made upstage, where they will have less claim on audience attention.

Note that the dramatically important character in a scene should tend to be slightly upstage, and possibly somewhat nearer the center of the stage, than the other character or characters.

CHECK–LIST FOR POLISHING MOVEMENT

1. Have you learned to keep your body poised, alert, ready? Have you learned to relax? To concentrate?

2. Have your major patterns of movement been clear, interesting, meaningful?
3. Have your movements been properly controlled, so as to focus the attention of the audience where it belongs? Have they seemed purposeful?
4. In your movement, have you begun to suggest the age of your character? His race, occupation, status, and the like?
5. Has your action been clearly related to the size and contents of the setting? To the other characters in the various scenes?
6. Has your character's behavior been clearly distinguished from that of the other characters? From your own behavior in ordinary circumstances?

EXERCISES FOR CHAPTER 3

I. In executing the following, try to develop a sense of easy balance:

(a) Stand comfortably erect, chest and head up, feet not too close together, hands on hips. Sway (from the ankles) slowly from side to side, then forward and backward, without moving the feet and without bending at the hips.

(b) Stand on the left foot and swing the right leg to the front and to the rear several times. Repeat slowly; repeat from the other side.

(c) With the weight on one foot and with the arms hanging freely (or extended horizontally), lift the other leg forward until it is at right angles to the trunk; then move it slowly down and back. As it passes the supporting leg, bend the trunk forward until the raised leg and the trunk are parallel with the floor.

II. Strive to develop a technique of conscious relaxation:

(a) Stand with the feet apart, legs straight. (If you prefer, support your hips against a wall, keeping your feet a short distance from the base of the wall.) Bend easily forward, relaxing the torso, arms, and neck. Sway the body from side to side, with the arms and head as loose as possible. Bounce the torso up and down several times, with the arms and head swinging loosely.

(b) Shake the hands at the wrists until the fingers are wholly relaxed. Relax the entire arm and swing it gently from the shoulder, letting the lower arm and the hand move freely.

(*c*) Let the head fall freely forward; slowly roll it to one side, back, and then around again to the front, being sure to stay as relaxed as possible. As the head reaches the front, let its own weight bear it forward to the chest. When you repeat, keep the muscles of the neck completely relaxed.

(*d*) Sitting on the edge of a table, swing the left leg freely forward and backward, then the right; alternate. Swing both freely from side to side in unison.

(*e*) Supporting yourself on one side by holding on to the edge of a table or to the back of a chair, swing the opposite leg forward and backward loosely from the hip joint; repeat from the other side.

III. Strive for freedom, economy, and precision; and remember, start with the right foot to the right, the left foot to the left:

(*a*) Practice stretching, bending, stooping and straightening, swinging from the hips. Practice walking, sitting, kneeling, entering and leaving the stage, crossing, turning, pacing.

(*b*) As you move about a stage or platform, have someone call out to you unrehearsed directions for moving, turning, stopping, pacing, approaching a chair, sitting, rising, standing, pointing.

IV. As you execute the following, try to develop your sense-awareness and your sense-memory. Focus throughout on the inner experience and not on your outward reaction to it; take your time, and *concentrate.*

(*a*) Imagine that you TOUCH: a hot platter; a piece of ice; lukewarm water; pieces of fur or velvet, satin or muslin.

(*b*) Imagine that you HEAR: a loud crash of thunder; a shrill sound in the next room; the rustle of a mouse or the buzz of a mosquito; a familiar melody; an unfamiliar voice; a dripping faucet near-by.

(*c*) Imagine that you SEE: an approaching storm, with occasional flashes of lightning; a passing friend; a skidding automobile; an approaching child who seems in difficulty; a four-leafed clover; an article that had been mislaid.

(*d*) Imagine that you TASTE: onion soup; sour pickles; grapefruit; mild custard; vanilla ice cream; cod-liver oil; pumpkin pie.

(*e*) Imagine that you SMELL: wood smoke; tobacco smoke; gasoline; turpentine; banana oil; roses; lilies; violets; a chest lined with cedar; a chest containing damp and rotting papers; a delicate cheese.

V. Repeat Exercise IV, but assume the directions now to read, "Imaginatively TOUCH, HEAR, SEE, TASTE, or SMELL, *and react to* the following." Try to recreate the "feel" of the sensation as vividly as possible; and as you respond outwardly to the inner stimulus, bear in mind that an audience may be watching (and trying to determine from what they see just what it is you have reacted to).

(*a*) Practice the several parts of the exercise before your group, and have your spectators guess from a predetermined list the item or items to which you reacted.

(*b*) Reach or look into a drawer that is at least partially hidden from those who are watching, and indicate by your reaction just what it is you find there.

VI. (*a*) Place a rehearsal table so that it extends just beyond a masking screen; stand behind the screen so that spectators can see only your arms, to the elbows. With and without real properties, perform various actions (including some of the sensory exercises listed above). Have the spectators guess the exact nature of your action, and judge as to its clarity and precision.

(*b*) Place a masking screen on each side of a portable blackboard; starting from behind the screen from the left, move across the open space between the legs of the blackboard, stopping behind the opposite screen. Have the spectators observe and judge your movements of leg and foot, as you assume the walk of various ages, occupations, states of health, and the like; as you walk over or through imagined sand, sod, mud, frozen ground, ice, and other surface materials.

VII. (*a*) In pantomime, shuffle and deal cards; light and smoke a cigarette or pipe; cut and prepare a vegetable for cooking; shine a shoe; eat a plate of soup; make a telephone call; unfold, read, and fold a newspaper.

(*b*) Do the same with dummy or substitute properties; with the genuine articles. Reverse the process, moving from real properties to substitutes to pantomime.

(*c*) Perform some of these actions with the hand and arm which you do not ordinarily use for the purpose.

VIII. With other actors and a teacher or director, work out

suitable patterns of movement for a character in one of the scenes in Appendix E, pages 173-215.

(*a*) Having introduced the scene to those in your audience who may not be familiar with it, walk through the movement you have planned, without lines but with precision as to gross bodily attitudes, stage positions, business, and characteristic detail. Do this with and without the other character in the scene.

(*b*) Repeat it just before and just after a complete acting out of the scene in its entirety. Have the spectators comment on your movement as such, and on its contribution to the whole.

IX. Repeat Exercises IV through VIII after you have covered later sections of the manual.

4 | Rehearsing the Part: Speech

Reading the Lines Naturally

The best criterion for the amateur actor's line reading may be summed up in a single sentence: Did the readings seem natural? Long hours of study and rehearsal, and the best of good intentions, will bring only limited success if a reading seems stilted and unconvincing. Good reading of dialogue has the quality and the effect of *real conversation*. It is lively and expressive, varied and interesting. A conversationally spoken line has a certain ring of the genuine and the normal which an obviously recited speech always lacks; it is without the exaggerated artificiality and the unreal monotony of mechanical declamation. A good actor gives the impression that he is thinking and uttering ideas for the first time, not merely repeating memorized words.

Such naturalness in the reading of lines is not so difficult to achieve as it may at first appear. Conversing in real life and reading lines in a play differ in degree rather than in kind; the mental action involved is much the same in both. In everyday conversation, the actor utters his ideas just as they are created in his mind. He speaks as he thinks, and the words come out as he thinks — a phrase here, a hesitation there, a word, a spurt of words, and so on. In delivering lines from a manuscript, on the other hand, the actor is repeating impressions that he has gleaned from a printed page. The point at issue, therefore, is that as an actor you must do in reading lines what you do in real conversation: just as your mind creates the thoughts you speak while you are conversing, so your mind must REcreate the thoughts you speak while you are reading lines. If you are like most students, your reading can be genuine, convincing, conversational only if your mind is actively present at the moment of utterance.

It is in this sense, then, that you are advised to read naturally. Nowhere has it been implied, of course, that you are just to "be yourself" on the stage, regardless of dramatic effect. If your day-by-day "natural" habits are to mumble your words or to mouth them overmeticulously, such faults must obviously be corrected. You can find here no blanket justification for habitually muffled or scratchy tones, or for a normally thin or breathy voice. Your lines on the stage must usually be clearer and more interesting than in real life. Hence, faults must be adjusted, meaningless or misleading details must be eliminated, and special points must be heightened for proper effect. But at no time must your speech seem stilted, mechanical, or artificial.

Expressing the Meaning

The first step in expressing the meaning of a character's lines is of course understanding them. At the very least this requires that you know the common meaning of all the words used in those lines. Use your dictionary as a guide, and be sure that you have mastered not only each literal and explicit meaning (that is, each "denotation") but each implication (or "connotation"). Don't take any chances; your grasp of detailed meanings must be complete, sure, unequivocal. Note that some words whose superficial meaning may at first seem evident might have been used in a special sense and that if you are careless you may miss the point entirely. Remember also that certain proper names, quotations, historical or literary allusions, and the like might have been given a specialized application.

But beyond such elementary problems of logical meaning lie other and no less important considerations. The basic job in expressing the meaning of a line is proper *grouping of the words* that it contains. That is to say, people normally do not speak in single words, but in groups of words. Each of these groups, in turn, expresses an idea, or a relatively complete part of an idea. To break up the idea by chopping its natural word group into separate words (or into unnecessarily small partial groups) makes for jerky reading that is both unnatural and difficult to follow. The single idea of "Go" may be taken as a simple illustration. In the author's manuscript, this idea may have been phrased, "Get out"; or, "Please leave the room"; or again, "Will you please leave this room at once." The number of words actually used here to express the idea varies from two to eight, although in each case the unit of thought is not the separate words, but the entire word group itself. With a sentence like the one above, "Will you please leave this room at once," a speaker does not think first and separately of *will*, then of *you*, then of *please*, then of *leave*, and so on; he thinks of all the words, grouped as a single idea. Similarly, in a longer sentence or group of sentences, one's thought does not move forward in a succession of single words, but progresses by word groups expressing single ideas.

From the standpoint of an actor preparing to read his lines, the number of words that are to be combined in a word group may vary considerably. The actor's decision must be based on the thought to be expressed and the circumstances under which it is to be uttered. If a character wishes to be impressive, or is speaking to someone who presumably has difficulty in understanding his ideas, he may use many and relatively short groups; under opposite conditions, few and relatively long ones. A typical word group, however, usually contains from six or eight to a dozen or more words, smoothly tied together and expressing a single idea. Each of these separate groups must be considered as a thought unit, regardless of its length, and each must be set off from its neighbors by a longer or shorter pause. Failure to group properly in the reading of lines results in falsified meanings and in dulled or warped characterizations.

But word grouping is only one step in adequately expressing meaning. In conveying ideas, an actor must be capable of centering, or focusing, attention on some parts of a thought unit, at the expense of other and less important parts. To give every phrase, word, or even syllable equal stress is merely to becloud the meaning. If the mind centers on important idea-carrying words and phrases, and relegates the others into the background of attention, expression is improved and heightened. Prominence is usually given (1) to *new* ideas at the expense of those that may have been mentioned before; (2) to ideas that show *change* or *contrast* in relation to others; and, in general, (3) to *main* ideas as opposed to parenthetical or subordinate ones.

In the following examples, not all of which are taken from dramatic literature, look for the key words and phrases that tend to establish the writer's or speaker's point. Assume that you are about to read the selections aloud, and plan to place proper focus of attention on the key words and phrases but to slip lightly over less important ones. Watch in particular for contrasts of any kind, and for *echoes* of what has already been said or established; the latter must of course be properly subordinated.

> A religion which rests on particular conclusions in astronomy, biology, and history may be fatally injured by the discovery of new truths. But the religion of the spirit does not depend upon creeds and cosmologies; it has no vested interest in any particular truth. It is concerned not with the organization of matter, but with the quality of human desire.
>
> WALTER LIPPMANN [1]

> Speak the speech, I pray you, as I pronounced it to you, trippingly on the tongue: but if you mouth it, as many of your players do, I had as lief the town-crier spoke my lines. Nor do not saw the air too much with your hand, thus; but use all gently: for in the very torrent, tempest, and, as I may say, whirlwind of your passion, you must acquire and beget a temperance that may give it smoothness.
>
> *Hamlet*

[1] From *A Preface to Morals*, by Walter Lippmann. By permission of The Macmillan Company, publishers.

LADY BRACKNELL: It is very strange. This Mr. Bunbury seems to suffer from curiously bad health. . . . I must say, Algernon, that I think it is high time that Mr. Bunbury made up his mind whether he was going to live or die. This shilly-shallying with the question is absurd. Nor do I in any way approve of the modern sympathy with invalids. I consider it morbid. I am always telling that to your poor uncle, but he never seems to take much notice . . . as far as any improvements in his ailments goes.   OSCAR WILDE, *The Importance of Being Earnest*

The civilized man has built a coach, but has lost the use of his feet. He is supported by crutches, but loses so much support of muscle. He has got a fine Geneva watch, but he has lost the skill to tell the hour by the sun. A Greenwich nautical almanac he has, and so being sure of the information when he wants it, the man in the street does not know a star in the sky.
RALPH WALDO EMERSON

I met a traveller from an antique land
Who said: "Two vast and trunkless legs of stone
Stand in the desert. Near them on the sand,
Half sunk, a shatter'd visage lies, whose frown
And wrinkled lip and sneer of cold command
Tell that its sculptor well those passions read
Which yet survive, stamped on these lifeless things,
The hand that mocked them and the heart that fed.
And on the pedestal these words appear —
'My name is Ozymandias, king of kings:
Look on my works, ye Mighty, and despair!'
Nothing beside remains. Round the decay
Of that colossal wreck, boundless and bare,
The lone and level sands stretch far away."
PERCY BYSSHE SHELLEY

When icicles hang by the wall
  And Dick the shepherd blows his nail
And Tom bears logs into the hall
  And milk comes frozen home in pail,
When blood is nipped and ways be foul,
Then nightly sings the staring owl,

"Tu-whit, tu-who!" — a merry note,
While greasy Joan doth keel the pot.

When all aloud the wind doth blow
   And coughing drowns the parson's saw
And birds sit brooding in the snow
   And Marian's nose looks red and raw,
When roasted crabs hiss in the bowl,
Then nightly sings the staring owl,
"Tu-whit, tu-who!" — a merry note,
While greasy Joan doth keel the pot.

Love's Labour Lost

In Shelley's poem, note how little weight the words "stand," "lies," and "appear" need to carry. The careful reader does not bear down on ideas whose meaning is naturally implied. Comment in this connection on the word "hang" (line one of the first stanza) and the word "blow" (line one of the second), in the Shakespearean song. Note also that articles, prepositions and conjunctions, and pronouns — with rare exceptions — do not take special emphasis in normal reading; such words as "I," "he," "to," "for," "and," "if," "an," and "the" are only too frequently overstressed. Ordinarily the nouns and verbs take first place in conveying meaning, with modifiers next.

On the whole, however, it is best not to look upon the process of centering as a mere stressing of chosen *words*. On the contrary, it should be regarded as a process of giving new (or contrasting or important) ideas prominence, or of bringing them into the focus of attention. If the actor sets his mind to putting the exact shade of meaning into the whole sentence or word group, then the stressing of individual words usually takes care of itself. Mechanical emphasis on certain words, on the other hand, may destroy the meaning as well as the natural sound of a line. No single formula is so effective for the actor in this connection as asking the simple question: "What, exactly, do I mean?" In line reading, a precise shade of meaning is rarely concentrated on a single word; usually, it colors the entire thought unit.

In the pages immediately preceding, expression has been considered principally as a matter of communicating logical or intellectual meaning. But a logically "correct" reading may still be unsatisfactory. Lines that are read as though barren of all feeling or that are given a mood which the author never intended are necessarily mechanical and dull on the one hand, or inaccurate and misleading on the other. A further step is obviously indicated. The actor must be responsive to the specific *attitude* that his character has assumed in the lines, and to the particular *emotional values* inherent in them.

If an actor were to read with grim seriousness lines clearly motivated as light and gay, or to deliver with extreme mildness and delicacy lines that call for bitterness and indignation, his gross misrepresentation would doubtless be spotted immediately, regardless of any purely logical exactness he might have attained. But just as important in every scene are less obvious emotional touches, to all of which the actor must be sensitive and responsive. Occasional lines are of course flat statements of fact, with no particular emotional color or significance. For each one of these, however, there are many others that depend for full expressiveness on the emotional overtones with which they are charged. Even in predominantly expository scenes, most lines stimulate, not merely inform. And the delicacy or playfulness, the vexation or regret, the earnestness or exaltation with which they stir the listeners is not something added from the outside like a sort of decorative *bric-à-brac*; it is something inherent in the dialogue and the scene.

As I have tried to indicate earlier, what a character "means" in a given line and a given scene depends in part on what he meant in the scenes which preceded and what he is going to mean in the scenes which follow. His true meaning depends not so much on the words he uses as on what he should be thinking and feeling, actually or imaginatively. The meaning in a line goes deeper than the particular phraseology that the author has used in stating the line; the meaning is colored by the character, by the character's personal motivations, and by the character's dramatic function in the scene.

It is a truism that one character may say the same words as another, but mean something quite different. To announce that one's horse has just made it "by a nose" takes on one coloration if the horse had been the preponderant favorite at 1-20, another if he had been 100-to-1 in the betting. The value which a character's reading sets on the words "Only a dozen or so" suggests whether he had previously expected one or ten or a thousand, and whether he was dealing with pearls or with grains of sand, with friends or with enemies, with wildcats or with locomotives. Assuredly, the same words may censure or approve, affirm or deny, deride or pay honor. The emotional quality or the character-motivation calling forth a line must color its meaning no less surely than its fundamental logical message; to assume a wrong attitude on a line (or *no* attitude at all) is as fatal to expressiveness as is false grouping or improper centering.

Insuring Vividness

So much for logical and emotional correctness. It must be apparent, however, that an actor's reading may be faithful to logical changes and responsive to attitude and emotion, and yet lack a certain conviction, a certain *vividness and color*. In the main, these qualities depend on the actor's personal warmth and vivacity. They depend as well on the constant variety and the cumulative interest which good reading demands. Probably the best way to insure such interest and variety from scene to scene is to maintain genuine *contact* with the other actors on the stage. A good reader of lines, like a good speaker, "thinks on his feet." As has already been emphasized, he functions as he does in earnest conversation. He has a firm grasp of the ideas he means to convey, and a strongly developed sense of communication. Such a reader listens, reacts, and responds: he answers back. In brief, he is neither hurried nor distracted; he is familiar with his lines and responsive to the meaning of his words as he utters them; and he has set his mind and body to active communication.

Another way to approach vividness is to recognize that a

well-read line has a ring of personal conviction. The character and the actor-as-character must seem to mean what they say, and they must say it with an individual and quite personal flavor. Several methods for attaining such vivid expression have long been used by conscientious actors. One method consists in temporarily paraphrasing a difficult line that doesn't ring true as the actor has been reading it. The language in which the line is phrased may seem unusual or unfamiliar to the actor, or it may express what are to him unusual or unfamiliar sentiments. Such speeches may be paraphrased into more familiar or more colloquial language, and rehearsed in this form until vivid and convincing expression is achieved. The tone and flavor of this expression may then be carried over into the original language, usually with appropriate and satisfactory results.

Consciously enlarging or intensifying natural contrasts is another way of insuring vivid expression. Although the reader is delivering a line correctly, it may seem monotonously even and flat; it may lack variety and contrast — what some actors have called "hills and valleys." The procedure here is to build up the height of the hills and to carve out the depth of the valleys. Where in a normal reading the actor's pitch had naturally although almost imperceptibly risen, he now takes it somewhat higher. Where it had naturally dropped a bit, he takes it even lower. If in one part of a speech he had naturally slowed down just a little, slowing this portion down even further will lend contrast to the other portions. In the same way, normal pauses may be lengthened, increases in volume may be intensified, and the like. The result is usually more colorful expression without any necessary sacrifice in naturalness.

If their lines lack flavor, some actors are aided by the simple device of "thinking into" a speech additional words and phrases that express appropriate implications. A few examples, built around the single line "I'm satisfied," will indicate various possibilities:

I'm satisfied (And by the heavens, I mean that. I really do!)

I'm satisfied (Satisfied! I'm no more satisfied than I was the last time.)

I'm satisfied (I've got to be. My cause is hopeless.)

I'm satisfied (For the time being. But wait and see!)

I'm satisfied (I'm satisfied, all right. I'm satisfied that you're a liar.)

The list could readily be made longer. Note that no mere trick of stress or intonation or voice quality, mechanically applied to these two words, could give them the precise shade of meaning and color that "thinking in" of specific implications can give them. Some actors, it may be added, go so far as to *speak* in such phrases as are illustrated above, later dropping the additional phrases when fully expressive readings have been achieved.

It should be stressed that good reading, in the sense employed throughout this chapter — i.e., intelligent and vivid responsiveness to meanings, both intellectual and emotional — is the basis of good characterization. If an actor's reading of well-written dialogue is "right," he has by that token achieved the sound beginnings of a character, so far as speech and voice alone are concerned. He is already individualized, up to a point, because his readings reflect the distinct individuality and the characteristic flavor which the author has written into his part. His patterns of rhythm, tempo, and even pitch and intonation are partially set.

Mechanical changes from, or additions to, the characterization which expressive reading naturally suggests must be made with caution. Even in playing unusual or eccentric roles, the performer should guard against the too-easy tendency to adopt artificial patterns of voice and speech that may destroy the aesthetic balance and proportion of his part. Unearthly squeaks or howls and a wholly unconventional delivery must surely be all right in their place; but they are not to be mistaken for believable characterization in either a serious or a comic play. Marked changes from the responsive actor's natural patterns are usually made only to insure projection of the part under performance conditions. The purely mechanical and artificial in speech is in most cases far easier to recognize from the audience than the mechanical and artificial in bodily action.

CHECK–LIST FOR POLISHING READING

1. Have you read your lines "naturally," suggesting the effect of real conversation? Have you maintained the "illusion of the first time"?
2. Have your thought units or word groups been clear and distinct? Are there too many groups? Too few?
3. Has prominence been given to new ideas; to changes and contrasts; to main ideas as opposed to parenthetical or subordinate ones?
4. Have you been fully responsive to specific attitudes that your character assumes from scene to scene, and to particular emotional values suggested in his speeches? Have the speeches in single scenes been consistent with the nature of your part as a whole?
5. Have you maintained lively contact with the other characters in the scene? Do you seem to "answer back"; to *mean* what you are saying?
6. Have you been able to develop or restore vividness and color by paraphrasing unfamiliar passages; by enlarging natural patterns; by thinking in transitional words or phrases; by any other device which is not a substitute for intelligent responsiveness?

EXERCISES FOR CHAPTER 4

I. Choose one of the prose selections in Appendix E, or a similar one supplied by your director or instructor, and analyze it for reading aloud.

(*a*) Read through the selection silently until the track of the thought is clear in your mind. Be certain of the meaning of each word as used in the present context, and of the significance of each name and allusion.

(*b*) Decide on the first and last word in each thought group, and examine the relation which each bears to earlier and later groups. Find the contrasts, echoes, restatements, amplifications, climaxes, and the like. Be able to defend your choice of thought centers for the various groups. Do not plan to substitute mere pounding or punching on certain words for subtle and proportionate focus of attention on certain ideas.

(c) Be sure that you sense the mood and attitude of each section, as well as the dominant feeling of the whole. Take every precaution against emotional wandering at the time of delivery.

(d) Note every opportunity for a natural pause, not only to allow your prospective audience time to assimilate the thought and feeling of what you have just finished, but to give yourself an opportunity to focus on what is ahead. Remember that pauses are useful when you need to call special attention to significant words or phrases, and are imperative when there is a break in continuity or when unrelated ideas must be set off from one another.

II. Analyze Arnold's *Dover Beach* (page 154 of Apenndix E), and prepare to read it aloud.

(a) Basically, what is the poem *about*? Love? The sea? The delights of a moonlit evening? A "note of sadness" suggested by the beach at Dover? In part it is about all of these, but there is a deeper, unifying pattern of meaning into which they fall, each in its own way and place. Define "Faith" as the author uses it here; start with a dictionary definition if you will, but add connotations and implications that you find in the context. Can you enrich your definition by knowing something about the author's background, temperament, or philosophical outlook? By considering the social and other changes that were shaking his contemporary world?

(b) In reading the poem aloud, be careful that you do not see and recreate the wrong image in such words as *shingles*. Watch your centering wherever there are inversions of normal word order; focus subtly but surely on the noun-ideas in *slow cadence, drear edges, furl'd girdle*. In the nineteenth line (beginning "Find also . . .") note that both *sound* and *thought* are in some measure echoes, not new ideas; and that in centering you will need to be cautious of their relation to *also* as well as of their relation to each other. Comment on other problems of centering or word grouping, including those problems accentuated by the poetical stress.

(c) Where does full expression of meaning depend on marked contrasts of major or minor importance? On sustained continuity, despite parenthetical elements of one kind and degree or another?

III. Prepare to real aloud Rupert Brooke's *Sonnet* (page 157).

(*a*) Comment in specific terms on the speaker's attitude toward the lover described in the poem.

(*b*) How would you characterize the dominant, unifying mood of the whole? How does your answer fit in with the mood ordinarily suggested by "Death," "shade," "loneliness," "mire," "stir unknowing"? Do not be so preoccupied with single lines or words that you fail to see the poem steadily and see it whole.

(*c*) The following has been offered as a précis of this sonnet: "No matter how we may ever be separated in space or in time, I shall never tire of knowing and watching you — you utterly delightful and lovely creature!" Is this a good précis? How would you improve on it?

(*d*) Note that although "Death will find me," in the first line of the poem, is *grammatically* the main clause, yet "tire of watching you" (which appears in a grammatically subordinate construction) is more directly concerned with the main *idea*.

IV. (*a*) Read the Stuart Chase selection (page 169) aloud. Without in the least slighting your analysis for intellectual and emotional content, focus this time on lively and colorful expression; work for the utmost vividness, variety, and range.

(*b*) Do the same for the Walter Lippmann selection (page 167), which, as you will soon observe, is quite different in nature. For the Macaulay selection, do the same thing.

(*c*) Do the same for one or more of the poems.

V. (*a*) Read aloud, from the book or from manuscrpit, one of the dramatic selections included in Appendix E. Pay special attention to expressing orally the intellectual and emotional meaning, and to insuring vividness; specifically use some of the suggestions and devices included in this chapter.

(*b*) Repeat this exercise after you have studied Chapter 5, on voice and articulation.

(*c*) Write out a critical judgment of similar readings by others in your group.

VI. Repeat some of the above exercises after you have studied Chapter 6, on characterization.

5 | Rehearsing the Part: Voice and Articulation

Voice Production

The actor's vocal mechanism, like his body as a whole, can be trained and developed. Given sufficient time and proper guidance, an amateur actor can do much to perfect the use of his voice; and, although expert voice production should not be confused with intelligent reading, yet poor voice quality or defective articulation can inhibit flexibility of response and interfere with projection of meaning at the time of performance. To forestall any basic misconceptions regarding the mechanism itself or regarding its normal functioning, it seems wise to review briefly the entire process of vocalization.[1]

All vocal tone is produced within the *larynx,* or voice box, when breath from the lungs is forced between relatively tensed and vibrating lips or folds, the so-called vocal cords. These cords are relaxed and separated during normal breathing, but are drawn together during vocalization; as the outgoing air is forced between them, their edges are set into vibrations which, in turn, set up sound waves that we recognize as vocal tone. The original tone produced in the larynx is then amplified and modified by the *resonators,* i.e., the passages of the throat (or *pharynx*), mouth, and nose. Finally, in a step that goes be-

[1] For fuller treatments, see Virgil A. Anderson, *Training the Speaking Voice* (Oxford University Press, 1942); George Dodds and James Dunlop Lickley, *The Control of the Breath* (Oxford University Press, 1925); and Robert Curry, *The Mechanism of the Human Voice* (Longmans, 1940). My own summary — together with other portions of the present chapter — has been prepared with the advice of Professor C. K. Thomas, of Cornell University.

yond voice production as such, the tone is formed into the
sounds of speech through the action of the *articulators,* i.e.,
lips, tongue, cheeks, teeth, jaw, and hard and soft palates.

The pitch of the sound produced depends on the frequency
or rate of vibration of the sound waves set up in the larynx.
Just as shortening, tightening, or decreasing the thickness of
a violin string causes it to vibrate with a higher frequency
when plucked or bowed and thus to initiate a higher tone, so
the vibration frequency and therefore fundamental tone produced by the vocal cords depend on variations in their length,
tension, and thickness. The student should note that the vocal
cords alone are responsible for the pitch of a sound, and that
therefore no other parts of the speech mechanism or of the
body as a whole can be brought into play to alter that pitch.
He should note also that the movements of the vocal cords
themselves are produced by involuntary muscles, and that control of these muscles is limited to the indirect control furnished
by a trained and sensitive ear. Hence, it is of vital importance
that there be no tension or strain in the throat during vocalization. If free action of the muscles within the larynx is inhibited
by pull and strain from without, the result is likely to be excessively high pitch and possibly a harsh or strident quality
as well.

At the same time, however, that the vibration of the entire
vocal cord is producing the frequency of a fundamental tone,
the cord is vibrating also in fractional segments and producing
related tones of higher frequency. These tones, called *overtones* (or harmonics or partials), determine the specific quality
which a sound at any given pitch will have. The selection and
intensification of certain partials at the expense of others —
and hence the particularization of the quality — takes place in
the chambers of the throat, mouth, and nose, in an action
known as resonance. Changes in the resonating effect of the
chambers depend on variations in size, shape, and surface texture, as well as in size of the opening.[2]

[2] The student can observe a simple manifestation of such changes if he
sounds a tuning fork over various jars, or if he plucks similar violin strings

If it is understood that the vocal resonators work effectively only as they are free to adapt readily to the requirements of changing tones (that is, free to become quickly and selectively attuned to a wide range of frequencies), the importance of muscular relaxation and flexibility, especially in the throat, becomes apparent. The freely functioning voice mechanism is capable of making, in response to meaning and to conscious effort controlled by the ear, a large number of adaptations within the resonators. Unless, however, the throat in particular is free from false tensions and is capable of instant adjustment, the characteristic normal differences of the various speech sounds as well as subtle and meaningful changes in the quality of the vocal tones must necessarily be lost. General richness and fullness of voice, usually ascribed to proper reinforcement of the fundamental and the lower partials, also requires an "open" and relaxed throat. If the muscles of the throat are tensed to the degree that the resonating surfaces are excessively hardened, the tone may become metallic or even strident.

Special attention should be paid to one adjustment within the resonating system that has so far not been mentioned: the valvelike action of the soft palate, at the junction of the mouth and upper throat. When the soft palate is fully lowered, it prevents air and therefore sound from passing into the mouth; and they then come out by way of the upper throat and nose, as in the sound represented orthographically by ng.[3] With most sounds, on the other hand, the palate normally rises and moves slightly backward, with the result that air and sound come out only through the mouth, the passage through the upper throat and nose being blocked. Weak or sluggish action of the soft palate leads to an excessively nasal

---

attached to boxes of differing kinds. He can get approximately the same fundamental tone in each case; but since various overtones are intensified in some cases and suppressed in others, the quality of the composite tones will differ appreciably.

[3] In only two other cases — m and n — does the sound normally come out through the nose; with these, however, the soft palate is not solely responsible for blocking passage through the mouth.

quality, since with such action the opening to the nose is too often not adequately closed. Flexibility and precision in palatal action can be developed or restored through exercise.

Many common difficulties in voice production are attributable to faulty breathing. Good breathing, so far as it concerns the voice, is without tenseness or strain, involving a considerable amount of physical freedom but a minimum of physical tension. In addition to a moderate rise and fall of the chest structure, there is an accompanying expansion and contraction of the body just above the waistline as a result of interaction between the diaphragm, the abdominal muscles, and the viscera.

The diaphragm, a dome-shaped, predominantly muscular sheet acting as the floor of the chest, rests on some of the organs below it in the abdominal cavity. In *inhalation,* the diaphragm contracts — i.e., flattens out and takes a lower position across the body — and crowds against the upper abdominal organs, which in turn press outward against the muscles of the waistline. This downward action of the diaphragm enlarges the chest cavity, which at the same time is enlarged in an outward direction by an "expansion" of the bony structure of the chest. As the chest cavity is thus enlarged, the air pressure within the lungs is reduced, and a relatively greater atmospheric pressure forces air in from the outside. In *exhalation,* the raised rib structure falls, partly because of its own weight, while at the same time the abdominal muscles crowd the viscera inward and upward against the diaphragm, forcing it back into its domelike position. The air is thus expelled from the lungs with a force that can be used in vocalization.

For the purposes of voice production, it is best to achieve enlargement of the chest cavity chiefly by diaphragmatic action (which is naturally accompanied by expansion at the waistline and by a slight raising of the lower ribs) and to depend on a minimum action in the upper chest. In the first place, as most voice teachers point out, there is less over-all effort involved in diaphragmatic as opposed to chest breathing; and the muscles concerned in this effort are farther removed in space and in function from those of the larynx and throat than are the muscles of the upper chest, and are thus less likely to interfere with vocalization. It is highly probable, moreover, that chiefly diaphragmatic rather than chiefly chest breathing best assures the full and deep breathing required for voice production. If the actor inhales no more deeply than in normal quiet breathing, his voice will be "gaspy" and will lack both variety and staying power.

Finally, diaphragmatic breathing, co-ordinated as it is with the action of the abdominal muscles, can assure not only deep but controlled breathing. In exhalation during vocalization, the tone must be supported against sudden fluctuations in breath pressure. This is most readily done by slightly delaying the lowering of the chest, which has been raised in some degree during inhalation, and by using the muscles of the abdominal wall to control the outgoing breath. Adequate breathing for singing or speaking demands a feeling of security, strength, and control at the waistline. The beginning actor can consciously develop such control by experimentation and exercise. Naturally, this work should not be done during rehearsal or line delivery; full concentration on the playing of a scene does not allow of special attention to breath and breath control, or indeed to any other technical matter.

Special Considerations

This necessarily brief account of normal voice production has emphasized for the student what he can and what he cannot do with his voice, and has indicated how he may make the most of the one he has. A normally "good" voice has been described as one which shows: (1) the firm support of controlled diaphragmatic breathing; (2) a free, smooth, and full response in the vocal cords, unimpeded by tensions from without; and (3) such readiness and flexibility of adjustment within the resonators as to insure (a) general fullness and richness of tone, and (b) reasonably precise discrimination in the matter of nasal resonance. A normally "good" tone, it has been assumed, is one that seems effortless and free; one that, as some teachers have put it, seems to flow easily through the throat as if there were nothing there to interrupt it. The prospective actor should note that the stage will also demand of his voice considerable variety and flexibility. Many roles will demand that he markedly extend his natural range, not only as to vocal quality but as to pitch and volume as well. If an actor is alert and responsive, a good deal of variety is possible within a relatively limited range, but in the long run a potentially wide range is almost indispensable.

Above all, the stage demands of an actor a trained and sensitive ear, capable of fine discriminations. If one's body is functioning normally, the voice responds freely though involuntarily to directions from the hearing mechanism; and most efforts to control the muscles of vocalization in any other way interfere rather than assist with the process. Sensitivity to distinctions in quality, for example, can be consciously developed by means of ear-training exercises, and such exercises are therefore a vital part of the average student's work. A student who has special difficulty in recognizing and controlling changes in quality or pitch usually finds that he can improve most readily by concentrating first on these characteristics in the speech of other persons and thus refining his discrimination, later turning to experimentation with his own voice. At this secondary stage, the playing back of phonograph recordings is a useful aid.

Several common faults in amateur acting are directly or indirectly the result of difficulties in voice production. The effect of "running down hill" during line delivery is one of these, since it can often, though not always, be traced to shallow or poorly controlled breathing. Too many actors attack each line with clarity and vigor, but then allow it to trail off as they near the end. Especially when repeated over a period of time, this procedure results in dullness or monotony. It has the further disadvantage that it regularly emphasizes the meanings in the beginning of a speech and regularly obscures those nearer the end. Such a pattern of emphasis is faulty not only because it is monotonous but because in most well-written dialogue the phrases near the end of a speech are likely to be most interesting and most important. Poor control is sometimes manifested also in jerky or puffy exhalation, which fails to supply the firmness and relative uniformity of support necessary during vocalization.

Another common fault is an excessively high pitch level. Occasionally there is need for the higher tones to express unusual excitement, fear, weakness, or loss of self-control. But a consistent use of high pitch may express these and similar emotional states when they are not intended; and in any case regular use of the upper pitch levels is monotonous and tiring to the audience. Most untrained voices, moreover, are thinner and poorer in quality in their upper registers, and without potential warmth and emotional coloring. For every voice there is a so-called optimum pitch, a general pitch level at which the voice seems best, both as to quality and as to maximum volume with minimum effort. This level is usually slightly lower than that of ordinary speaking. If you are a typical amateur, you will do best to depend normally on your middle and lower-middle range of tones, where your voice is naturally fuller and richer than elsewhere and far more pleasant and interesting to listen to.

A judicious avoidance of extremes in volume seems the best policy. Some actors, striving to make themselves understandable, have a tendency to "shout," a tendency that must be carefully suppressed. Mere loudness must never be confused with clarity; when an audience reports that it cannot hear the actors, it may mean that it cannot understand them. If a series of speeches is difficult to comprehend from the house, excessive volume will rarely remedy the situation. The actors in the scene may discover that indistinct enunciation or perhaps some fault in the reading accounts for the trouble. Or they may find that inadequate resonance is chiefly responsible. A thin, unresonant tone has no carrying power; and what the speeches may lack is not more volume (in the sense of more breath energy and wider vibrations in the vocal cords) but fuller resonance, at the same volume as before.

On the other hand, the level of volume must never be so low that even good enunciation, expert line-reading, and full resonance do not carry to every point in the house. Nothing is quite so disconcerting to an audience as not being able to hear certain portions of the dialogue. Even if these are relatively unimportant to the action, the listeners naturally feel annoyed, and their annoyance is often carried over to later and perhaps better scenes in the performance. Then, too, while a listener is puzzling over some part of the dialogue that he has missed (or possibly questioning his neighbor about it), he may be failing to grasp an important section which follows the part in question.

Articulation

Since the articulators (lips, tongue, teeth, jaw, and hard and soft palates) can be readily examined, and to a degree observed in operation, the actual formation of speech sounds out of the raw material of breath and tone is relatively easy to modify and control. Full details on articulation are not within the scope of this manual; [4] just enough information and comment will be offered here to give the beginning actor a working basis for study and improvement, and to lend clarity to the special applications which immediately follow. The traditional classifications of speech sounds — into vowels and consonants, voiced and voiceless (or breathed) sounds, and oral and nasal sounds — will be useful for present purposes, even though strict lines of demarcation cannot always be maintained.

The distinction between *oral* and *nasal* sounds has been made in an earlier section. Nasal sounds, it will be remembered, are those for which the air escapes only through the nose (i.e., [m], [n], [ŋ] [5]), the exit through the mouth being

[4] Anderson, *op. cit.*, offers a standard treatment of the subject; such volumes as W. Norwood Brigance and Florence M. Henderson, *A Drill Manual for Improving Speech* (Lippincott, 1939) are also of considerable use to the beginner.

[5] Phonetic symbols have been used throughout most of this chapter to represent sounds; in a few cases orthographic indications have been substituted. Where there seemed to be special reason for doubt as to the exact sound meant, key words have been included. The phonetic symbols used are listed

blocked. Most English sounds are oral, with the air in this case escaping only or chiefly through the mouth. All vowels and most consonants are *voiced* — i.e., are formed out of air which has become voice or tone because the vocal cords have been set in motion (e.g., [ɑ] or [z]). A few consonants are *voiceless,* or breathed, in that they are "noises" formed in the vocal passages after the air has passed by the vocal cords without setting them into motion (as in [s]).[6]

The distinctions between *vowels* and *consonants* is traditionally held to depend on the degree of obstruction (principally in the mouth) that is offered to the outgoing breath. During consonant formation, voiced or unvoiced breath is partially stopped or obstructed as it passes out the upper vocal passages, as in [m], [f], [t], [d], and [g]. With vowels, voiced breath is sent out with relatively little obstruction, the vowel's distinctive character being due principally to the size and shape of the mouth cavity, as in [i] (bee), [e] (rate), [ɑ] (ah), [o] (go), and [u] (tooth). The formation of the separate vowel sounds is determined chiefly by the (1) position and (2) relative slackness of the tongue; although, as observation will show, such factors as the angle of the jaw and the degree of lip-rounding account for some of the difference. Thus the vowel sound [i] is formed with the tongue bunched forward in the mouth, and high; [u] with the tongue back in the mouth and high. For [ɔ] (jaw), on the other hand, the tongue is back but low. For all three of these sounds, the tongue is relatively tensed; for other vowel sounds (e.g., [ɪ] and [ʊ], those in *hit* and *put*), the tongue is relaxed. Many combinations of tongue

at the end of the chapter in a table reproduced from the Kenyon-Knott *Pronouncing Dictionary of American English* (Merriam, 1944); the Kenyon-Knott volume is the only adequate pronouncing dictionary of American English, and the serious student would do well to own a copy.

6 The student can readily distinguish between such sounds as [s], [f], and [p] (voiceless) and [z], [v], and [b] (voiced) by holding his finger on his "Adam's apple" while he is forming the sounds; the distinct vibrations felt in the case of the voiced sounds will be absent during the formation of the voiceless ones. A finger held lightly along the side of the nose will sense vibrations when a nasal sound is being formed, but no vibrations in the case of even a voiced *oral* sound. Since the nasal cavity is shut off in the latter case, and is not operating as a resonator, there are no vibrations localized there.

position and tension are of course possible. In all, about eighteen separate vowel sounds (including those in *yet, sang, full, further,* and *above*) are recognized as standard English sounds. Several additional sounds are *diphthongs* — i.e., represent a gliding together of two sounds to form a single composite sound within the limits of one syllable (e.g., [aʊ], [aɪ], and [ɔɪ], as in *how* and *house, thy* and *thine, toy* and *toil*).

Six English consonants ([p], [t], [k] and [b], [d], [g]) are *stops* (or *plosives*), so called because they are formed by stopping the breath in its passage through the mouth and then releasing it with a slight explosion. The sounds of [p] and [b] are equivalents; that is, both are formed by a lip obstruction, though the former is voiceless, the latter voiced. The following diagram illustrates other relationships:

	Formed by lip obstruction	Formed by tip of tongue on upper gum-ridge	Formed by back of tongue on soft palate
Voiceless stops	[p]	[t]	[k]
Voiced stops	[b]	[d]	[g]
Voiced nasals	[m]	[n]	[ŋ]

Thus the three nasals are formed by obstructions at the same places as for the stopped consonants, though of course the palatal position is different for the nasals.

But the nasals differ from the stops in another way: like all consonant sounds except the stops, they are *continuants* — i.e., the breath out of which they are formed is merely impeded, not stopped, and their duration may therefore be prolonged. Examples of continuants are the so-called fricatives (like [f], [v], [s], [z]), which depend upon audible friction caused by squeezing air through a narrow opening; and the so-called semi-vowels (like [w] and [j], the consonant sounds in *we* and *ye*), which are relatively open and unobstructed. These and other continuants vary not only as to whether they are voiced or breathed, but also according to the place of their articulation (lips, tongue and teeth, tongue and palate, and so on). By observation, experimentation, and study, the student can readily make sure how the consonants [7] are formed, and can check up on those which cause him difficulty, or those which he may need to modify for dialect roles.

But the actor is interested not only in separate sounds or words and their formation, but in sounds in action — the sounds of connected and flowing speech. If he enunciates too carelessly, he may be difficult to understand; if too carefully, he may seem unnatural and affected. He must usually strike a happy medium between an enunciation that is careless, slipshod, and unintelligible and one that is overprecise, labored, and falsely emphatic (in that it places stress on important and unimportant alike).[8]

The phenomenon of *gradation* in vowels is of special significance here. In isolated or stressed positions, *you* and *do* may be pronounced with the [u] vowel, as in *tooth*; in unstressed positions in connected speech the vowels may be reduced from their original value to weakened forms. Thus, in the sentence "How do you do?" the *you* — depending on a permissible range as to rapidity and formality of speech — may be pronounced not with the vowel [u] at all, but with (1) one approaching [ʊ], the vowel sound in *put,* or (2) one approaching [ə], the first vowel in *above* and the second in *custom.* In the same sentence the first *do* may go through somewhat the

---

[7]   TABLE OF CONSONANT SOUNDS

Voiceless	[p] [t] [k] [f] [s] [ʃ] [θ] [hw]
Voiced equivalents	[b] [d] [g] [v] [z] [ʒ] [ð] [w]
Voiceless (no voiced equivalent)	[h]
Voiced (no voiceless equivalent)	[m] [n] [ŋ] [l] [r] [j]

For further details on consonant or vowel sounds, see the references listed in an earlier footnote to this section.

[8] In this connection, see pages 41-45 under "Expressing the Meaning." An overprecise enunciation, in which each word or syllable is given equal value, is just as bad as a slovenly enunciation; sometimes it is worse. Overprecision in reading dialogue is both unnatural and uninteresting. Moreover, it destroys normal word grouping and interferes with proper focus on the relatively important meanings in the lines.

same set of gradations. In the polysyllabic words *enough* and *deceitful,* the [i] (*bee*) sound which the first syllable in each would require if it were fully stressed becomes normally [ɪ], the vowel sound of *hit.* The vowel sounds in *a, the, and,* and *or* rarely require strong pronunciations; and in *and,* for example, there are several possible degrees of weakening, according to its position and use in connected speech.

It must be understood that the weakened or obscured forms are not half-legitimate substitutes (for the strong forms) in unstressed positions, but are essential to the demands of normal English speech. "Ee-nough," "dee-ceitful," "How-doo-yoo-doo," and "Put-a-chair-on-THE-platform" are in ordinary circumstances distortions of natural English patterns, and should not be resorted to in a mistaken attempt to achieve effectiveness or clarity of speech. Although vowels in fully or relatively stressed positions should not be falsely obscured, those in unstressed positions should be allowed a proper degree of weakening.

On the whole, the ancient rule-of-thumb "Take care of the consonants and the vowels will take care of themselves" is poor advice. It is true that consonants are mainly responsible for abstract and mechanical clarity of enunciation; but the vowel sounds (as well as some of the continuant consonants) give the voice its quality, its carrying power, and its emotional expressiveness. The actor can afford to pay undue attention to neither at the expense of the other, though certain weak consonants (e.g., [f], [p], [t], and [θ]) must be articulated clearly. Faulty articulation in general can usually be traced to sluggishness or carelessness in using the speech mechanism; or to excessive rapidity or jerkiness, often associated with unnecessary muscle tensions and poor co-ordination. Simple exercises can be used to restore flexibility and precision in the use of the articulators.

Several distinct types of faulty articulation are worthy of the actor's attention. Among these are the blurring or muffling of vowels in general, as in the substitution of "Amurrican" for *American* and in the confusion of the vowel in *will* for that of *wool* or the vowel in *good* for that in *gird*. Ordinary vowels should not be stretched into diphthongs, as in "keh-ump" for *camp*, "skoo-ull" for *school*, and "law-erd" for *lord*. A reverse tendency, to shorten diphthongs into simple vowels (e.g., [a] for [aʊ] in *bound* or *hours*), should also be resisted. The too-frequently omitted consonant sound [t] should be restored in such words as *mental* and *mountain,* and the [n] sound should not normally replace the [ŋ] sound in "ing" words. On the other hand, there should be no false insertions or restorations, as in "ath-a-lete" and "umbarella" or in the spelling-pronunciations which include the *t* in *Christmas* and *hasten.* False re-stressing of normally weakened vowels has already been mentioned. Naturally, articulation difficulties due to the actor's own provincial or foreign speech must be cleared up in some measure for ordinary roles.

Some of the faults listed above — and they are only samples — are bad on the stage because they interfere with clarity; some because they call special attention to themselves; some, perhaps, for both reasons. Any habit which calls undue attention to voice or pronunciation *per se,* and therefore distracts attention from the dramatic action, is of course a potential trouble-maker. It should be recognized that an affected or meticulous enunciation is just as offensive in this respect as an unnecessarily careless or slovenly one, an excessive preoccupation with vocal "beauty" or "quality" just as offensive as no concern with the voice at all.

Pronunciation

The choice between what are commonly called speech standards is at times a critical one for the actor. It is well known that there is in this country no universal standard of pronunciation. Three broad types are usually recognized by phoneticians: (1) New England or Eastern (*E* in the Kenyon-Knott dictionary); (2) Southern (*S* in Kenyon-Knott); and General American or Midwestern or Northern (*N*), this last extending

— except for the South — roughly from the west bank of the Connecticut River to the Pacific Coast. There are many variations in and between these three types, but three outstanding differences may be noted. First is the omission by Southerners and New Englanders of the "r" sound after a vowel in the same syllable, as in *further*; in standard Northern speech this "r" is usually pronounced.[9]

A second distinction is based on the pronunciation of the vowel in such words as *class, laugh,* and *path.* Northern and Southern generally uses [æ] here, as in *sang*; but New England uses [a], a vowel that approaches [ɑ] as in *ah.* A final distinction (entering also in the matter of "stage English," of which more later) concerns the vowel in such words as *not, stop,* and *hod.* Most sections of the country tend to use [ɑ] as in *ah* for this purpose; but Easterners prefer [ɒ], a sound that approaches [ɔ] *(jaw).* Naturally there are other differences and other kinds of difference (e.g., intonation patterns), but these are some of the principal ones.

So far as the stage is concerned, the point at issue is not that one American standard, as outlined above, is superior to the others, or that a single standard compounded of these is possible or desirable. The point is that any actor who fails to approximate the standard of his fellow-actors has a special, attention-catching dramatic value, whether this is intended or not. All other things being equal, the production of a play based on the pronunciation standard of Boston is not necessarily better than one which uses the standard of Nashville or Baton Rouge, of upstate New York or the Pacific Coast; the production is merely different. A native of Boston, playing in Iowa or Missouri in a cast chiefly from the Midwest, or a native of New Orleans transplanted to Syracuse, has a distraction value in the ordinary play that cannot be discounted. Indeed, the distraction value may be used in a positive way, as in the casting of such a person as the only "outsider" or

---

[9] Sometimes (as suggested by the spelling "mother-r-r-r") the effect of such an "r" is exaggerated by turning the tip of the tongue back toward the palate and by tensing the back of the tongue, this being a retroflex or inverted "r."

"stranger" in a group otherwise made up of members of a single family or community.

Partly as a means of minimizing the effect of such regional discrepancies, "stage English" [10] was for many years widely accepted as a theater standard. Approximating as it does South British in all essentials, stage English is still suitable to certain plays with a strongly British flavor; and it is appropriate, though not essential, to some types of drawing-room comedy. The experienced and versatile actor should ultimately master it, as he should master various American and foreign dialects. However, in most contemporary plays, which bear only the dimmest relationship either to London or to the drawing room, stage English seems merely out of place. Particularly when used by amateurs, moreover, it may seem slightly affected and therefore distracting in many communities throughout the country.

In any case, the speech of all the actors in any typical production should — except for special cases — meet on some sort of common ground as to standards of pronunciation. That is to say, actors playing members of the same neighborhood or the same family need not have identical pronunciation patterns; but their speech should be relatively free from unmotivated regional or dialectal limitations, generally similar to that of the other actors, and reasonably acceptable to the audience for which they are playing.

Certain outstanding speech characteristics (that is, of individual actors) that clash with the norm for the cast can usually be softened or lessened in their effect, though not necessarily removed, during rehearsal. The retroflex "r," for example,

10 This includes most of the characteristics of New England pronunciation, described above, plus other characteristics patterned chiefly on South British pronunciation. Insofar as it does follow South British, it favors a much greater weakening of vowels in unaccented syllables than is usual in this country; examples are the pronunciations of *library* and *theater* as something approximated by the spellings "lib'ry" and "thitteh." Other strongly British characteristics are an exaggerated lip-rounding of the vowel in *law,* and a pronunciation of the vowel in *patch* and *bad* which approaches that of the vowel in *vetch* and *bed.* Daniel Jones, *An English Pronouncing Dictionary* (Dutton, 1943) is a good reference for British pronunciation.

can be modified without being "dropped." *Hard* or *mother* need not remain "har-r-rd" or "mother-r-r" in cases where this conflicts with the norm, or in cases where it seems merely unpleasant. If, during the formation of "r" in these words, the student avoids undue tension at the back of the tongue and raises the tip slightly toward the upper gum ridge (without either tapping against the gum ridge or curling the tip backward), the unpleasant effect can be lessened and the marked departure from the norm can be weakened — especially if the vocalization is not unduly prolonged.

The abnormal pronunciation called for in dialect parts and plays is a difficult and time-consuming problem. For this reason many organizations postpone the production of predominantly dialect plays until a highly flexible cast and ample time for experimentation and drill are available. On the whole, it is best for stage purposes to suggest or approximate a dialect rather than to imitate it in detail, if only for reasons of intelligibility. If certain outstanding characteristics of the dialect are focused upon and if these are used subtly and consistently, no distraction or lack of clarity need result. The general *effect* of the dialect is what is required, not a mechanical reproduction.

In some cases the significant characteristics are chiefly sound substitutions — e.g., voiced for voiceless sounds or vice versa (as [z] for [s]); [t] or [s] for [θ] as in *thin* and [d] or [z] for [ð] as in *then*; the vowels in "sheep," "git," "syme," and "fate" for those in *ship, get, same,* and *feet.* Often, however, sound substitutions alone, without subtle changes in speech rhythms or intonations, will not do the job. A few authors, notably Synge and Yeats, have happily caught dialectal rhythm and melody in the very diction and sentence structure of their dialogue; here the actor's problem is not so much what to do with or to the dialect, as what not to do, lest he spoil it.

By far the best procedure for the actor is ordinarily to plan on direct observation of those who speak the dialect with which he is concerned; whenever this is impracticable, listen-

ing to phonograph recordings and studying phonetic trans-
criptions may be resorted to. Unless the play's director has had
phonetic training, the actor may need to consult a phonetician
— preferably one who is aware of theater requirements and
limitations.[11] A few actors may need the warning that the
Pat-and-Mike of the vaudeville or burlesque stage and their
counterparts will not serve as models under ordinary circumstances.

CHECK–LIST FOR POLISHING VOICE AND ARTICULATION

1. Has your breathing been predominantly diaphragmatic-abdominal? Has it been deep enough for adequate voice production?
   Has it been well controlled?
2. Has your throat been free from strain or tension, allowing full
   and smooth response in the vocal cords during vocalization?
3. Has your voice been resonant enough for normal warmth and
   richness of tone, as well as for adequate projection? Has it been
   free of artificial nasality?
4. Have you developed sufficient vocal variety? Have you been
   able to extend your range, especially as to quality and pitch?
5. Has your reading been free from the extremes of meticulous or
   slovenly enunciation? In particular, have you avoided restress-
   ing normally weak syllables?
6. Have you learned to use your articulators with flexibility and
   precision, without slighting vowel or consonant sounds yet
   without calling attention to either?
7. If your role is a straight one, have your pronunciation patterns
   approximated the norm for your cast? If it is in dialect, have
   your patterns been intelligible and at the same time not distracting?

[11] Some assistance may of course be had from books and articles, and from
various dialect dictionaries and handbooks of phonetics. Among the journals,
American Speech will doubtless prove interesting as well as useful. *A Manual
of Foreign Dialects,* by Lewis Herman and Marguerite Shallett Herman (Ziff-
Davis, 1943), is the most complete volume on the subject, though trained
phoneticians have found it uneven as to accuracy; Charlotte Crocker, Victor
A. Fields, and Will Broomall, *Taking the Stage* (Pitman, 1939) contains a
section on foreign and other dialects.

EXERCISES FOR CHAPTER 5

I. For relaxation:

(*a*) Repeat some portions of Exercises II and III of Chapter 3, especially those concerned with the head and neck.

(*b*) Let your chin drop, and simulate a yawn; if you can induce a real one, so much the better. With the "feel" of a yawn in your consciousness, sound and sustain the vowel [a] (*ah*). Repeat with [u] (*tooth*).

(*c*) Sound the vowel [a] with the yawn in mind, and with the mouth open as far as possible without strain; now alternate this with a hard clenching of your teeth.

II. For breathing:

(*a*) Lie flat on your back and place your right hand on your chest, your left hand at the waistline; relax, and breathe quietly. Do not attend to the breathing as such, but focus on your hands. Since in this position the chest cannot rise and fall easily, your breathing will be chiefly diaphragmatic; and your left hand will rise and fall with the expansion and contraction of the abdominal muscles, while your right hand will remain relatively motionless.

(*b*) Take a standing position, and place the hands as before. Breathe slowly and easily, allowing the chest and waistline to expand and contract together; then, on every other exhalation, contract the waistline *before* contracting the chest. Repeat, but expand and contract the waistline three consecutive times before dropping the chest at all. Try to get and retain the "feel" of diaphragmatic-abdominal breathing.

(*c*) With a minimum of chest action and a maximum of diaphragmatic action, take a full breath, easily but fairly rapidly, and then release it gradually; repeat several times. Then, on every other exhalation, quietly sustain the sound [f]. Keep the sound production steady, and avoid sudden fluctuations in volume. Do not exert specific pressure on the outgoing breath; just relax. Repeat with [s]; with a quiet [a].

(*d*) Now, by exerting pressure on the breath column, increase the volume of [f], sounded as in (*c*), above. How much have you had to decrease the duration? Try for both volume and duration with [a], at about the middle of your pitch range. Keep the tone steady; don't waste any breath. Keep your throat muscles relaxed, your chest relatively still, and your abdominal muscles active. On [ɑ], gently swell and later diminish the volume, consciously using the breathing muscles to start, stop, and control the tone.

III. For vocalization:

(a) Intone [ɑ], as in II, (d), above. Focus now on making the tone rich, full, and strong, without changing the pitch. Experiment with various levels of volume, and with the crescendo-diminuendo technique described above. Try to change the volume without thinning out the quality. Go up and down a scale of an octave or more, without altering volume or resonance; have others in the group check up on you.

(b) Using [ɑ] and [u] (and later [m]), again at the middle of your range, deliberately try to produce what you would describe as a "thin" or "weak" tone; a "harsh," "metallic" one. Alternate these with normally full and rich tones. Compare notes with others in your group. Play back recordings of such exercises as the present one, and comment on your control of tone production and resonance.

(c) With breath firmly supported and throat relaxed, intone the consonant sound [ŋ] (-ing). Keep the tone rich and full, and consciously note the "feel" of its vibrations. Now alternate slowly between [ŋ] and [ɑ], trying to avoid any change in the fullness of resonance (except of course in the shift from nasality).

(d) Read aloud one of the poems in Appendix E (e.g., the excerpt from "Childe Harold"). Read it slowly at first, intoning or chanting it within a very narrow pitch range. Try to carry the "feel" of full resonance, developed earlier on single sounds, over into this reading. In successive readings, gradually restore the tempo as well as the intonation patterns of a more normal expression; but retain the voice quality of the earlier readings.

IV. For articulation:

(a) (Lips) Exaggerate the lip movements as you repeat: "ee-oo-ee-oo," etc.; "ah-oh"; "ee-ah-oh." Alternate with minimized and exaggerated lip movement.

Pronounce rapidly: "mee-mee-mee," etc.; "woo-woo-woo"; "fah-fah-fah"; "bub-bub-bub."

(b) (Tongue) Open your mouth, extend your tongue, and hit rapidly against alternate sides of your mouth.

Tap the tip of your tongue rapidly against the gum ridge; sustain the breath but relax the tongue so that the outgoing breath "rolls" the tip of the tongue rapidly against the gum ridge.

Repeat slowly, then rapidly: "lah-lah-lah," etc.; "tuh-tuh-tuh"; "kuh-kuh-kuh"; "tuh-kuh-tuh-kuh"; "three-throo-three-throo."

(c) (Jaw) Move your lower jaw from side to side, effortlessly but fairly rapidly.

Repeat rapidly, opening the mouth wide on "ah": "oo-ah-oo-ah," etc.; "fah-fah-fah"; "wah-wah-wah"; "ahwah-ahwah-ahwah"; "bah-goo-bah-goo."

(d) (Soft palate) Alternate, at first slowly, then more rapidly: "mmm-ah-mmm-ah," etc.; "mmm-aw"; "mmm-oo"; "zzz-ah"; "zzz-aw"; "zzz-oo"; "zzz-mmm"; "zzz-nnn"; "zzz"- [ŋ].

Intone a series of non-nasal sounds (or a sentence containing no nasals — e.g., "The gray sea, the dark sky, the cheerless house — all suggested the very spirit I sought to avoid.") with a finger held against the side of the nose. You should feel no marked vibration.

Now read such material with the nose held tightly shut; if there is a feeling of breath pressure in the nose or the effect of muffling on the sounds, your palatal action is faulty.

Try the same material (and alternate with material that does include nasal sounds) with a small mirror held under the nostrils. Note that no mist can form on the glass unless some of your breath is escaping through the nasal passages.

(e) Repeat various tongue-twisters (e.g., Esau Wood sawed wood, She sells sea shells, Peter Piper picked a peck, etc.), first slowly and then at increased speeds, maintaining intelligibility throughout.

Do the same with the Gilbert and Sullivan selections in Appendix E, pages 158-59; with others.

V. For pronunciation:

(a) Have several members of your group read aloud, in succession, a prose selection from Appendix E, focusing on expression and intelligibility though not on pronunciation as such. Make careful notes on major and minor differences in pronunciation; discuss with the group which of these differences might have a dramatic value in performance, and consider how they might be modified, if necessary, to approach the norm for the group as a whole.

Footnote to Phonetic Alphabet on facing page

' Placed above and to the left of a syllable, indicates primary stress on that syllable
, Placed below and to the left of a syllable, indicates secondary stress

The Phonetic Alphabet

VOWELS

Symbol	Spelling	Spoken Form	Symbol	Spelling	Spoken Form
i	bee	bi	ʊ	full	fʊl
ɪ	pity	ˈpɪtɪ	u	tooth	tuθ
e	rate	ret	ɝ	further	ˈfɝðɚ *accented syllable*
ɛ	yet	jɛt			*only, r's sounded*
æ	sang	sæŋ	ɜ	further	ˈfɜðɚ *accented syllable*
a	bath	baθ *as heard in the East,*			*only, r's silent*
		between æ (sang)	ɚ	further	ˈfɝðɚ *unaccented syllable*
		and ɑ (ah)			*only, r's sounded*
ɑ	ah	ɑ	ə	further	ˈfɜðə *unaccented syllable*
	far	fɑr			*only, r's silent*
ɒ	watch	wɒtʃ *between ɑ (ah) and*		custom	ˈkʌstəm *unaccented syl-*
		ɔ *(jaw)*		above	əˈbʌv *lable*
ɔ	jaw	dʒɔ			
	gorge	gɔrdʒ	ʌ	custom	ˈkʌstəm *accented sylla-*
o	go	go		above	əˈbʌv *ble*

DIPHTHONGS

aɪ	while	hwaɪl	ju	using	ˈjuzɪŋ
aʊ	how	haʊ		fuse	fjuz
ɔɪ	toy	tɔɪ	ɪu	fuse	fɪuz

CONSONANTS

Symbol	Spelling	Spoken Form	Symbol	Spelling	Spoken Form
p	pity	ˈpɪtɪ	dʒ	jaw	dʒɔ
b	bee	bi		edge	ɛdʒ
t	tooth	tuθ	m	custom	ˈkʌstəm
d	dish	dɪʃ	m̩	keep 'em	ˈkipm̩
k	custom	ˈkʌstəm	n	vision	ˈvɪʒən
g	go	go	n̩	Eden	ˈidn̩
f	full	fʊl	ŋ	sang	sæŋ
v	vision	ˈvɪʒən		angry	ˈæŋ·grɪ
θ	tooth	tuθ	l	full	fʊl
ð	further	ˈfɝðɚ	l̩	cradle	ˈkredl̩
s	sang	sæŋ	w	watch	wɒtʃ
z	using	ˈjuzɪŋ	hw	while	hwaɪl
ʃ	dish	dɪʃ	j	yet	jɛt
ʒ	vision	ˈvɪʒən	r	rate	ret
h	how	haʊ		very	ˈvɛrɪ
tʃ	watch	wɒtʃ		far	fɑr
	chest	tʃɛst		gorge	gɔrdʒ

(*b*) Read a speech of some length from a drawing room comedy or a play of some other kind of strongly British flavor; for example, choose a speech by Lady Bracknell or Algernon in *The Importance of Being Earnest*, or one by a member of the "upper classes" in a play by Shaw or some other contemporary British dramatist. Read it first with your own normal, day-by-day pronunciation patterns. Then read it with your version of South British, giving careful attention to expressiveness, consistency, and intelligibility. Compare notes with an experienced actor or director, and check against the Jones dictionary and phonograph recordings of South British. Apart from sound substitutions and weakening of syllables, watch your patterns of intonation.

★★★★★★

6 | Rehearsing the Part: Characterization

In the early chapters of this manual, the actor was advised to look upon character-building as a three-fold task, embracing the separate but related steps of conception, embodiment, and motivation. It was suggested, however, that the order in which the steps are here listed indicates in only a rough and general way the sequence which the actor can ordinarily follow in building his character. Naturally enough, most of the "conception" does grow out of the pre-rehearsal analysis and the early rehearsals; much of the "embodiment" does take place soon thereafter; and full "motivation" does come chiefly as the later rehearsals approach. But rigid or literal adherence to any such notion of sequence would be aesthetically and psychologically unsound, as well as wasteful of time and energy.

Ultimately, there can be no cut-and-dried division between the analytical and the creative, the objective and the subjective, the preliminary and the final, in characterization. The point is, rather, that as time goes on the fragmentary and the sketchy become progressively more complete. Some details are changed and others are added; early and necessarily tentative notions are modified, refined, and enriched; and substance appears where there was only skeletal framework. But analysis and study cannot be arbitrarily restricted to the first week or two of preparation. Patterns of speech and movement cannot be hurriedly decided upon at one stage in the process and then forever neglected; nor can motivations be hastily tacked on, as it were, just before the dress rehearsal.

The broad outlines of your characterization, then, should be tentatively set during the first stages of preparation. Your conception of your character should be fundamentally though not unalterably decided upon, and its outward form should be approximated, as early as possible; and both should be based in large part on the clues which the author has written into his manuscript. Sooner or later, however, as the preceding chapters have already suggested, such clues must be supplemented by your own contributions, adapted from your own day-by-day experiences. Indeed, your keenness in observing the habits of those about you bears a direct relation to your ultimate success as an actor.

Choosing and Adapting Details

Almost every player who has tried to write seriously about the nature of his task and about his method or technique has stressed this point. Although the beginner is urged in passing to turn to books, to music, and to the graphic arts for models and inspiration, he is directed primarily to the daily life of all kinds of people in all kinds of circumstances. He is advised to observe and remember details in the church and the hospital; in the farm, the factory, and the marketplace; and in the breadline and the subway as well as in the lobby at the opera. To be sure, he is not asked to store up these details so that he may some day merely imitate or reproduce them as a kind of novelty act or trick, or as a kind of outer decoration which he can apply to the surface of the character he has conceived. But he is urged to record them with accuracy and discrimination, so that he may later adapt and combine them for use in motivated expression.

Thus, remembered details of posture, voice, and gesture can sometimes be fitted into the patterns of objective characterization that you are gradually developing. A certain frown, a way of carrying the hands, an unusual hunch of the shoulders, a distinctive tone of voice are simple examples. Each of these, observed in others, may seem to suit the character you are studying; and each, properly used, may help to give your character the appearance, the spirit, or the significance that you want. On the whole, you will do well not to borrow from performances you have seen in the motion picture or legitimate theater. External patterns used by professional players, when they are reproduced by amateurs, are likely to seem awkward, superficial, and stereotyped. Whenever possible, look to life rather than books, to people rather than other plays or other actors.

Although in most plays it is dangerous to conceive of characters as merely types and not as individuals, note that the policeman, the banker, the blacksmith, and the schoolteacher do have outward mannerisms characteristic of their professions. They walk, stand, move, wear their clothing, perhaps fix their hair in a somewhat specialized way. Various races and nationalities and various stations in life, regardless of the occupations involved, can sometimes be differentiated on a similar basis. Typical patterns of speech and movement can also be observed in habitually sick persons, or in other persons usually isolated from normal society.

Whatever details you do choose, in speech or in action, to establish your character's outer personality, be reasonably sure that you maintain the same general effect throughout. Each gesture or bit of business should fit in with others that have gone before and with the total characterization you have decided upon. Choose only the most telling and most typical details from the many that will doubtless suggest themselves, and then make the most of the relatively few you have retained. A limited number of selected characteristics, clearly conceived and accurately presented, will make possible the unity and the coherence demanded by all artistic expression.

In any case, attitudes, gestures, or mannerisms that ultimately find a place in your outer characterization should — like details of costume, properties, and make-up — be conceived of and used as an extension of your own expressive powers. If you conceive of them as merely outward decoration or disguise, or never learn to use them as anything more than that, they will tend to interfere with rather than assist projection. It follows, then, that special costumes, spectacles, beards, and the like must be "worn" intelligently and imaginatively. It follows also that the use of them (sometimes in the form of temporary substitutes) must become habitual over a relatively long period of rehearsal. Otherwise their handling will seem uncertain, and prompted by chance or by outer rather than inner compulsion.

Naturally, specific habits and traits observed in others will have to be adapted carefully for use in your particular play. They will have to be adapted, for example, to suit your voice and your physique. Two quite different persons cannot play the same part in exactly the same way; and a manner of wearing the hair or of gesturing with the arms which might be suitable for one type of individual would not do at all for another in the identical role. The particular postures that you use, moreover, depend in part for their clarity and significance on what the *other* characters are doing at the same time. If your choice in these matters is too close to, or conflicts too sharply with, the habits which the other actors have assumed, mutual adaptations will necessarily have to be made. Again, certain obvious character traits that might be "right" for some scenes or some plays may seem to be out of place in others. Details that proved suitable in a serious drama might be too depressing or too distracting if used by the same general class of character in a lighter play. The final success of your experiments in characterization will thus depend not only on the keenness of your observation but on your resourcefulness in adapting the details you have observed.

There are of course other adaptations prescribed by the general circumstances of theatrical presentation. Details of characterization, whether derived in whole or in part from real-life observation, must be so modified as to project readily from a stage to an audience under theatrical conditions. The sight-lines and acoustics of a typical theater make certain adaptations imperative, as do the special arrangements of individual settings, property plots, and lighting installations. A gesture, mannerism, or movement which might be a natural and significant reaction in one's own living room, in the classroom, or, let us say, on a picnic, may not be clear and meaningful under stage conditions. Some of these patterns might need restriction, others enlargement or heightening; all might need modification in some degree.

A stage movement should of course normally be played toward the house, and should not ordinarily be hidden even in part by large properties, individual actors, or groups of actors, and so on. Allowance must be made also for the dramatic value resulting from the exact area on the stage (in relation to the other actors and the various units in the setting) in which or toward which the action takes place. In the living room at home a characteristic movement might be made in any one of several directions, with no loss or gain in general expressiveness. On the stage a movement in one direction may insure clarity, interest, and emphasis, although the same pattern in another direction or in another relationship to the ensemble would be weak or meaningless, if not both.[1] Note that an outward pattern of movement or characterization which has been adapted to theatrical purposes need not suggest — that is, need not suggest because of the adaptation — either insincerity or artificiality. If the actor is properly concentrating, he can vivify and motivate a movement which he has "learned" to make in one direction practically as readily as one he might make in another.

Special problems of adaptation arise with violent movement of any sort, and with extremes of laughter or sobbing and the like. Whole "speeches" in real life might be sobbed into one's handkerchief, into one's palms, or onto a sympathetic shoulder. On the stage such an emotional reaction and the lines that accompany it must be projected to an audience, which cannot forgive an actress who lets the handkerchief get in the way. If sobbing on someone's shoulder is the natural outward ex-

---

[1] For further discussion of these points, see Appendix A, pages 113-17.

pression of a correct inner emotional state, then the actress must so modify her outward reaction that, without seeming false or mechanical, she can reach beyond the footlights.

Indeed, whenever movement must be combined with dialogue, certain mutual adaptations are inevitable; and the way in which the two are correlated can itself add to, or detract from, the expressiveness of either. An extremely restless or excited character, for example, may need to make frequent and broad movements, to pace, and to rise and sit a number of times in even a short scene. Such action serves primarily as a means of establishing character and state of mind. No opportunity should be missed, however, to make it serve the additional purpose of lending particular force and significance to certain lines. In general, a movement or gesture should accompany, or if possible *precede*, the point it emphasizes or illustrates. For dramatic clarity and emphasis, the normal sequence is: (1) thought, (2) movement, (3) speech. This sequence allows the actor to gain and hold the attention of the audience, and gives his message a sense of climax. A reversal of the sequence is not only anticlimatic but unnatural, for persons in everyday life normally move or gesture just before they speak.

Apart from delineation of character or state of mind, certain bits of movement or business must frequently be introduced to make a scene seem "easy" or "natural." Some characters, especially when they are chiefly engaged in listening for relatively long periods, may need to knit, to sew, to draw on a pipe, to whittle, or to pursue some other minor activity suitable to their characterization. Business of this sort, unobtrusive in itself and seemingly unimportant, adds naturalness to what otherwise might be a slow and awkward scene; and as a result the actors do not seem to be merely "making speeches" at each other. Here again, the action, if it is skillfully adapted to suit the needs of the scene, can serve the additional function of pointing up the dialogue and generally controlling the attention of the spectators. If a character is sewing, she can stop when she disagrees, point with her needle to emphasize her objection, start up again when she has been momentarily satisfied, slow down when she is particularly interested, pause frequently to listen, and spend at least a portion of the time with her hands relaxed on her lap.

Supplying Adequate Motivations

On the stage as in our day-by-day existence, gestures and intonations and meanings change as *purpose* changes. In deciding how to handle most external actions, therefore, the actor must focus as early as possible on the reason behind the actions, on the purpose that will give them specific form and meaning. A good actor, it is worth repeating, does not move down right or cross up left merely by chance or impulse; and he does not move only because his play script baldly states that he should. He seeks the "why" of an action first, and makes the "when" or the "how" grow out of his understanding of the "why."

If the author has omitted any specific mention of the reason for an action (or has stated it only by implication), it is obviously your task to search for the proper motivation and if necessary to jot it down in your manuscript. Having memorized such a line as "It's about time for me to be leaving" and the accompanying stage direction "He crosses to the door and leaves the room," you are only partially ready to act. You will be farther along if you discover, or are told, that your character is bored or discouraged or angry. But you will fully understand your exit only if you have found or supplied an adequate explanation for the boredom, the discouragement, or the anger. And unless it is based on such understanding, your action may seem neither clear nor logical to the audience.

But the influence of motivated reactions on the stage reaches far beyond the matter of simple crosses and exits. In the tiniest detail as well as in the most complicated dramatic pattern, the precise nature of one's line-reading and one's pantomime is conditioned by the underlying motivations. This element in acting is so essential — and it is so frequently overlooked, neglected, or misunderstood by the beginner — that it is worthy of further analysis and discussion here. It may be well to begin with physical actions of the simplest kind. Let us assume a stage direction: "He reaches out toward the wall." If the actor does not know why he is reaching, or has forgotten and is thinking of something else, or is just not concentrating, his action is wasted. If he "just reaches," the movement will lack interest, naturalness, and meaning.

You can test this out for yourself with interesting and, I think, useful results. Have one of your group (who is not forewarned as to the nature of the experiment) stand at the front of the room, and direct him to make a clear and specific but unmotivated physical action — in this case, "Reach out toward the wall." Then supply a purpose for his action (e.g., to turn on the overhead light), and after a while supply another. Observe how the action now takes on meaning, color, and conviction, even though the experiment is unrelated to a dramatic context. Note also the way in which the "how" of his action changes with your directions, though the "what" remains fundamentally the same. You might direct him to reach out merely to straighten a picture on the wall, or to keep the picture from falling under the stress of some overenthusiastic pounding in the apartment next door; or to examine a book on a wall-shelf because he thinks it is handsome, or because he wishes to borrow it, or because he recognizes it as his own. In each case, the "how" of the external action would stem from the "why."

Now ask another of your group to look for "something" on the stage. After a few moments, direct him to look on the floor of the stage; to look for a *pin*; to look for a valuable pin, a borrowed or stolen pin, a pin whose loss or recovery may have serious social consequences. Allow some time to elapse between directions, as you gradually supply additional details and as you complicate the situation. Now add the urgency of a time-limit, assuming that the loser or the owner or a policeman is due to arrive within a few minutes. As before, the basic action, the "what," changes and develops with each new motivation. Note, however, that in the experiment with the pin you have gone considerably further than you did in the earlier one: to the simplest cues for action within the immediate situation, you have added *context,* motivating circumstances. Thus the outer form of an action is conditioned, on an elementary and obvious level, by the character's immediate purpose; and it may be conditioned further by attendant or preceding circumstances.

Now conceive of a scene in which your character is a young man about to borrow his father's car for the evening; and assume his lines and certain basic stage directions to be given. Note that once you had learned these, you would still know in only the most limited sense how to play the scene. Just how you would speak and move and react depends on *why your character wants the car* (e.g., to perform some duties which his father had recently required of him, or to drive some friends to a near-by place he suspects to be "out-of-bounds"); and on various *motivating circumstances* (e.g., the fact that a request for the car for that evening had previously been denied, or the presence in the room of an older brother with whom he had recently had a major quarrel).

Whether the play in which the scene might appear was a light comedy or farce, or was a relatively serious drama, would of course be a further conditioning factor, and there would be others as well. But the hypothetical scene in itself does suggest how, on various levels and in various ways, motivations determine the outer form of dramatic action. The literal sense-meaning of dialogue and stage directions can only partially dictate the way your character behaves in general, and the way he moves and speaks in particular. Indeed, if you are to develop skill as an actor, you may have to revise your conception of how language operates, of how meanings are communicated in written and especially in oral discourse. For reasons which cannot concern us here, much language teaching in the schools has been restricted to a somewhat limited view of grammar and to a study of word-meanings based primarily on the authority of common usage. It is not my purpose to question the validity of dictionary definitions, founded as they are

on historical derivations and on the meanings ascribed by a
majority of the best writers and speakers. But I do wish to
stress that meanings are too often conceived of as fixed and
static, and that too little attention is commonly paid to the
context in which words and phrases and sentences appear.

A good dictionary can supply for the student only the literal
sense-meaning of a word (important as that is, to be sure), or
at best some of the connotative and metaphorical meanings
that have come to be generally recognized. What it cannot
supply is the additional meaning determined by the intellectual and emotional context of which the word or phrase is a
part. As soon as a word is used with other words in a sentence
or a sentence is used with other sentences in a longer unit, it
"means" something else, and possibly something more, than it
meant to begin with. And once the mood, the purpose, and
the attitude of the writer or speaker are also considered, the
word or sentence "means" something else again. That is to say,
the functional form, tone, tempo, and intonation pattern are
determined in large part by the underlying motivations. If this
generalization is valid for the simplest passage of non-dra-
matic prose or poetry, it is all the more so for dramatic passages, in which sense-meanings are commonly merged with
highly complicated variations of mood, intent, and attitude.

In line-reading, then, as in physical movement, motivation
enriches meaning, and the actor cannot expect significant results from a purely external approach; he must search always
for inner purposes, as these are qualified by attendant circumstances.

One method of bringing motivations to bear on one's role is
to analyze each scene in terms of dramatic *desire*, in terms of
the question: What, specifically, does each character want in
the scene? According to the Russian systems stemming from
Stanislavski,[2] the answer should be given in terms of an "(inner)

[2] See especially *An Actor Prepares* (Theatre Arts, 1936). For brief accounts
of methods based on Stanislavski, see Lee Strasberg, "Acting and the Training of the Actor," in *Producing the Play* (ed. John Gassner, Dryden Press,
1941) and I. Rapoport, "The Work of the Actor," in *Theatre Workshop*, vol.
I, no. 1, October, 1936.

A grouping from Thornton Wilder's MERCHANT OF YONKERS, as produced by the Penn State Players.

OEDIPUS THE KING, as staged by the Northwestern University Theatre.

Scene from a revival of AT YALE, by
the University of Virginia Players.

KING LEAR at the University of Minnesota Theatre.

action" or "task" and should be stated as an action verb. Thus a character's task in a given scene may be to make his family understand, to avoid an issue or an argument, to protect his sister or his wife, to assert his faith, or to demand recognition and so on. If the task is properly conceived and if in playing the scene the actor concentrates on the task rather than on what he is saying or doing *per se*, the line-reading and the external action may in large part take care of themselves.

Naturally enough (as some of Stanislavski's followers would be the first to point out), the actor must evaluate each task and its fulfillment in relation to the larger units of the play and in relation to the play as a whole. This is precisely why the preliminary analysis called for in Chapter 2 — which to some beginners may have seemed of purely academic interest — ultimately takes on functional importance of considerable magnitude. The play's structure, dominant mood, style, and theme frequently have an immediate bearing on how a character "acts" in an individual scene. In the same way, a character's specific desire in a given scene must be weighed against his basic desire for the whole play, and must be viewed in relation to his main line of action. Whether a character is meant to support or oppose the protagonist, whether he is meant to face the play's fundamental conflict or to evade or obscure it, is ultimately a matter of practical, and not merely theoretical, importance. In a reverse direction, of course, rehearsal scenes may require breaking up into still smaller units from time to time; and the dramatic desires and tasks proper to these units must then be integrated with those for the larger scenes and for the play as a whole.

"Feeling" the Part

In finding your character's motivations, however, and in translating them into action, you must usually move well beyond the confines of the play. For the richest understanding of your character, you must call upon your own experience, your own knowledge of people and families and communities. Plays, it is usually said, are larger than life. On the other hand, they are significant or amusing or appealing chiefly as they are based on human nature in the "life" that most of us know. Plays do not copy life; they adapt it, put it in order, magnify it. But they must rarely lose sight of it.

The memory of your own loneliness or weariness or discouragement, for example, in a situation somewhat similar to that described in your play, can be a potent aid to characterization. Suitably adapted to the dramatic situation and to the personalities involved, such an incident could be made genuinely helpful. The same might be true of the recollection of an incident which you had observed though not necessarily experienced. Your memory of a family or neighborhood crisis, and of the varied reactions of persons of different backgrounds and interests, could be the basis of some of your best work. The final motivations that make a scene on the stage believable and memorable frequently come from the actor's personal understanding of human nature in everyday situations.

But how strong are these real-life ties to be? Just how, and to what degree, can an actor carry over from remembered experience a feeling or an attitude and apply it to his role? While he is acting, does he "feel" basic emotions; and if so, in what sense are they real? These questions are by no means new, and they are not to be settled with scientific precision. Historically, interest in the problem of emotion in acting has at times taken the form of a debate over the so-called actor's paradox — that is, the fact that an actor must in some sense and to some degree feel deeply if he is to arouse an audience, yet he must not feel too deeply lest he lose his self-control.

Diderot, in his *Paradox of Acting* (1770), took the extreme position that the successful, the "sublime," actor must be completely insensible to emotion. In *The Actor and His Art* (originally published about 1880),[3] the French actor Coquelin supported a somewhat similar view, thereby starting a controversy

---

[3] (George Allen and Unwin, London, 1932), tr. Elsie Fogerty. Appears in English also in another translation.

that lasted for a decade or more; among others, Sir Henry Irving was articulate in opposing Diderot and Coquelin. The British critic and playwright, William Archer, collected and edited a great deal of testimony on both sides of the question, ultimately publishing his results in *Masks or Faces?* (1888).[4] This book, which takes a middle position in the controversy, is still of interest and value to student-actors. Although its practical usefulness today is limited somewhat by inevitable shifts in audience taste and opinion and by a certain vagueness of terminology within the book itself, it remains a stimulating point of departure for a study of the actor's paradox.

Closer to our time, some theories of acting have been predicated on a belief that the actor should feel more or less "real" emotions during performance. On the whole, the followers of Stanislavski, whose influence has been widely felt in the past few decades, incline to this position. Memory of emotion ("affective memory") plays a large part in the Stanislavski system. Through affective memory, Stanislavski believed, a properly trained actor can experience such emotions as fear and rage on the stage, and can call them up at will. He does this, not by recalling the emotion directly or by trying to remember its outward form, but by concentrating on certain details or objects associated with a previous real experience which embraced the emotion. By technical means that I have barely sketched here, the actor is urged to recreate feelings which for the most part he had once experienced.

Other theorists or critics of acting have questioned this aspect of the Stanislavski system or have independently arrived at a basically opposite view. Theodore Komisarjevsky, himself a distinguished Russian artist, seriously doubts whether emotions experienced in the past and recalled by the kind of psychological associations recommended by Stanislavski are not too weak to be of any practical use on the stage. He stresses also that in his view the nature and the quality of a character's emotions in a given scene of a given play depend much more on the artistic style and form of the specific play than Stanis-

4 (Longmans, London, 1888).

lavski seemed to admit.[5] Other Russian artists and critics of the theater have joined Komisarjevsky in making these objections, as well as others that are not in point here.

Dr. Lorenz Kjerbühl-Petersen, a German actor and scholar who has served as Director of the Mannheim Theater, states flatly that most actors do not feel in performance the specific emotions of their parts for more than a few moments at a time.[6] He bases this judgment not only on his own experience as an actor and director, but on the testimony of actors and critics representative of most European countries and of theatrical generations covering more than a century. Along with certain other actors who have tried to analyze their approach to the art, Dr. Kjerbühl-Petersen does draw attention to a generalized emotional attitude — a kind of general excitement called up by the scenery, the other actors, and the audience — which may well be necessary to a vivid performance. Some of our own contemporary actors bear witness to the presence and the efficacy of this emotional excitement during most performances.[7]

Using the Imagination

Any such emotional attitude, however, is quite a different thing from the specific emotions of a role. What the present discussion has so far omitted is the function which creative imagination can fulfill in the portrayal of emotional life on the stage. Much of the difficulty here — about "feeling the part," about the actor's paradox, about "genuine" emotions that are too weak or too strong — is resolved when one conceives of an imagined, theatrical reality. If stage emotions are real in any sense, they are imaginatively real, first, to the actor who portrays them, and second, to the audience who for the moment

[5] See his *The Theatre* (John Lane, London, 1935) and *Myself and the Theatre* (Wm. Heinemann, London, 1929). Note that in making these criticisms Komisarjevsky does not denounce the Stanislavski system *in toto*; on the contrary, he, like numerous other critics, finds the system sound and practical in many of its applications and significant in its influence.

[6] See his *Psychology of Acting* (Expression Company, Boston, 1935), tr. Sarah T. Barrows.

[7] See, for example, Morton Eustis, *Players at Work* (Theatre Arts, 1937).

believes them. "Feeling the part" thus becomes creating, in terms of experience *and* imagination, along channels indicated by the play and by its form and style. "Reality" becomes an aesthetic reality, which a given audience in a given theatrical era will accept for a given play.

The fundamental issue is probably not how much or how little emotion is required, not how strong or how weak the emotion is to be, but how vivid is its imagined creation. In this view, a strong sense of observation, a keen responsiveness to various kinds of stimuli, and an active imagination are among the actor's most desirable subjective qualities. Stimulated and guided by the author's manuscript, the actor selects from remembered experience details which his imagination fashions into behavior-patterns expressive of his role. The outward form of such patterns, both of speech and of movement, is shaped in part by the demands of plot, characterization, and other elements within the play, in part by such considerations as unity, focus, and balance in the director's design; and this outer form is gradually learned through constant repetition in rehearsal. Ultimately, the actor gives it warmth, conviction, and additional meaning by concentrating on inner motivations.

Certainly the actor must ordinarily *believe* his fictional situation to be, for the moment, true and real. He must accept imagined stimuli and react as though they were genuine. He must in some sense take canvas and beaverboard for walls and doorways, must see outside his stage window not stage braces and floodlights but a vista bathed in sunshine or drenched in rain. He must pretend that his character's desires and frustrations and emotions are creatures of fact and not of fancy. But, to repeat Lambert's often-quoted phrase, he must keep a "warm heart and a cool head."

The successful actor is in most plays primarily a character, and thinks a character's thoughts, feels a character's emotions, and looks at the world through a character's eyes. But there is in him at the same time a sort of second man, who looks out for the actor without interfering with the character. The second man, the actor-as-actor, thinks of his director's design, checks the precision and the timing of his speech and movement, makes adjustments to compensate for the unexpected, and is generally aware of audience reaction. The two — actor-as-character and actor-as-actor — must normally be in balance. If as an actor you lose yourself in your character, your performance may be uncontrolled and unreliable, to the detriment of teamwork and projection. If on the other hand you focus too strongly on your acting at the expense of your character, your performance may be lifeless, artificial, and unconvincing.

The symbol or key that will bridge for the actor the gap between real and imagined experience necessarily varies with individual persons, as it varies with individual emotions, individual scenes, individual plays. At times the bridging is natural and direct, growing immediately out of the actor's personal experience; at other times it is borrowed and possibly adapted from an apparently unrelated personal incident or from the experience of other people. Richard Boleslavsky's suggestion that the young actress who had never committed murder must certainly have felt at one time like slaying a mosquito is well known.[8] Helen Hayes testifies that, in preparing her role for the motion-picture version of Hemingway's *A Farewell to Arms*, she found a key to her character's emotional nature in something Conrad had once written about somebody else: a girl who had "the terrible gift of intimacy." For a scene in *Coquette*, Miss Hayes used as a symbol the impact which she had once felt when she saw a news-photographer's picture of an accident.[9] Burgess Meredith reports that he carries into certain scenes in which he is required to be very angry an I'd-like-to-sock-you-in-the-eye "feeling" that serves him well. An actor of his acquaintance once used as the key for a suicide scene a re-creation of the feelings he always experiences just before he steps into a cold shower.[10]

To this degree, then, an actor need not genuinely feel an emotion, if only he succeeds in making his audience feel it and believe in it. Actor-as-character and actor-as-actor, imperson-

---

[8] In his *Acting* (Theatre Arts, 1933), p. 44.
[9] Eustis, *op. cit.*, pp. 26-27.   [10] *Ibid.*, p. 98.

ator and interpreter, he must usually steer a middle course between completely deceiving or deluding his audience on the one hand, and merely presenting his own (and not a character's) personality on the other.

CHECK–LIST FOR POLISHING CHARACTERIZATION [11]

1. Given the basic requirements of your part in the play, what have you added to your characterization by way of objective details observed in persons about you? From the many details that may have occurred to you, have you selected and refined a relatively few outstanding and typical ones? Have you suitably adapted them to your play, to your production, and to theatrical conditions in general?

2. Have your external patterns of speech and movement been clearly motivated? Has the "why" been as apparent as the "what" and the "when"?

3. In dialogue and in action, has the "how" been conditioned by the "why"? Have you been aware throughout of underlying motivations, not only in an immediate situation but in its larger context as well?

4. Have you been able to enrich your playing of the character by focusing on the dramatic desires and tasks within the several scenes? Have you related your conception of each scene to your own and your director's conception of the play as a whole?

5. Again given the basic requirements of your part, what have you added to your characterization from subjective experience remembered from real-life situations? Have you learned, imaginatively, to bridge the gap between real and dramatically believable emotions and experiences?

6. Have you kept a warm heart but a cool head? Have you learned to maintain a proper balance between actor-as-character and actor-as-actor, avoiding the extremes of either an uncontrolled and unprojected performance or a mechanical and unconvincing one?

EXERCISES FOR CHAPTER 6

I. Review Chapter 3, Exercises V through VII. Focus not only on developing sense-awareness and sense-memory, but on enlarg-

[11] To supplement this list, review questions 4, 5, and 6 on page 50; questions 4 and 5 on page 36; and questions 7, 8, and 9 on pages 21-22.

ing and refining your powers of concentration. Note that some of these exercises check on the keenness of your observation as well.

II. Devise for your group other exercises intended to stress accuracy of observation. These may be based on or suggested by the following:

(a) Over a period of time, observe the gross bodily attitudes of representative mechanics, farmers, office clerks, clergymen, and others. Do you find in these groups characteristic details that might be typical of the class rather than of the individual? List and evaluate any such details, especially in so far as they might later be used on the stage in motivated expression. Do not be satisfied with stereotypes borrowed from stage, screen, or popular magazine.

(b) Make similar observations of extremely old persons. Again avoiding stereotypes, can you find in head, shoulders, torso, knees — in action and at rest — tensions or stresses or weaknesses which may be typical of age? Which of them could most easily and readily be assimilated into a total characterization? Which of them would tend to project? Which are fundamentally masculine; feminine?

(c) Make a report on what, in normal situations, people tend to do with their hands, their legs, and their feet. Observe them in a living room, at an amusement park, at a church service, at a political meeting, at work and at play. Observe, if possible, the immigrant foreigner, the Mayflower descendant, the Yankee, the Southerner, the Westerner; the educated, the highly skilled, the illiterate, the unemployable. Report on your observations and compare notes with others in your group. In making any generalization, bear in mind what adaptations to theatrical conditions you might have to make if you were to put your observations to use on the stage.

III. Devise also individual and group exercises in concentration comparable to the following:

(a) Try the childhood game of "Up Jenkins." Seat two teams, each with a leader, at opposite sides of a long table. Team one passes a fifty-cent piece back and forth underneath the table. At the command "Up Jenkins" from the leader of team two, all of team one place elbows on the edge of the table, with all hands clenched; at the command "Down Jenkins," all of team one slap hands flat on the table. Team two's leader, with the advice of his observant mates, is empowered to ask that certain hands, suspected of covering the coin, be lifted. The object is of course to locate the coin as early as possible from observation of team one's actions, conscious and unconscious.

(*b*) Try "Simon says." In this game a leader calls directions to a group spread out in standing position before him (e.g., thumbs up, thumbs down, thumbs out, hands overhead). The directions are to be followed exactly and without hesitation only when the leader prefaces his command with "Simon says"; if anyone follows a command not so introduced, he is "out." The leader attempts to confuse the group by following all directions, whether properly introduced or not; and he may complicate the game by executing directions other than those he has given.

(*c*) A member of your group is required to assimilate the content of one prose selection while another member is reading another selection aloud; or the entire group is required to focus on one selection while two are being read aloud.

IV. (*a*) Pass a small stick throughout the group. Accept it and handle it as: a peppermint stick; a piece of ice; a dirty piece of coal; a catnip mouse; a pet white mouse; an injured bird.

(*b*) Pick up, handle, and carry an empty traveling bag as though it were: empty; lightly filled; heavy. Carry it away as though it contained something: you were sure you didn't want; you might want if you were right about the contents; you wanted very badly. Combine these and other specifications in various ways.

(*c*) Stand comfortably and at ease for a minute or two, as though listening to a conversation which did not directly include you for the moment; now sit down on a plain rehearsal chair, treating it as though it were an easy chair. Using the same rehearsal chair, sit down and get up several times, assuming that the chair is familiar; unfamiliar; heavy; light; comfortable; uncomfortable; rickety. Then stand behind the chair for a moment, and finally move it across the stage as if to join a group conversation; as before, change your conception of the chair from time to time. Ask your group to criticize your pantomime from various points of view.

V. (*a*) Ask one of your group to pound on a door and/or rattle the knob (i.e., with no further directions or purposes given). Now add, in succession, such motivations as: to see if anyone is there; to wake a heavy sleeper; to test the strength or security of the door. Comment on the precision or accuracy with which the "how" follows the "why." Devise other exercises of a similar nature.

(*b*) Ask several members of your group to say one or more of

such words as: *sea; gun; schoolhouse.* Now have them think silently
of one such word for several minutes, gathering associations and
enriching the content; then let them speak the word with vivid
awareness of its context. Comment on the differences between the
original and the final delivery of the same word; between the varying final versions of the same word. Ask various members of the
group to say one or more of such phrases as: "all set"; "a warm
day"; "about a dozen." Then let them distinguish between different connotations of or different motivations for the several phrases
— e.g., all set (in concrete), all set (during rehearsal), all set (to
go); a warm day (in February), a warm day (in July); and so on.

(*c*) Ask one of the group to sew, that is, "just sew"; then ask
her to focus, to concentrate, on the sewing. Now add a succession
of additional directions and contexts: sew as before, but focus on a
character in a scene; focus on the character's listening in a scene
(under various given circumstances); use the needle and the sewing to point up the listening or the interrupting or the speaking in
which the character is engaged. Later ask the same person to
sew as a vaudeville pantomime and gag — e.g., sew her fingers together, work them up and down on the thread, and the like. Comment on fundamental differences between the several units in the
series.

VI. Have everyone in the group learn the lines for one or both
of the characters in the following experimental exercise. Then play
it under varying conditions and with varying backgrounds and
attitudes, as indicated below.

ONE: Hello!
TWO: Hello.
ONE: Well!
TWO: Well, what?
ONE: How are things?
TWO: Just about as usual.
ONE: I didn't expect to find you here.
TWO: But you have. . . . Of course, I could say the same of you.
ONE: Are you going to be busy from now until dinner?
TWO: Not exactly — not busy.
ONE: Wouldn't you like to talk for a while?
TWO: I might. For a while, anyway.
ONE: Right!
TWO: Right.

(*a*) In so far as possible, play it straight — with no overtones or implications, no attention to immediate motivations or preceding circumstances, no specific characterization. Try to deliver the sense-meaning and only the sense-meaning. (Note that any arbitrary stiffness on the part of one of the actors, or such factors as excessive movement, may *give* it meanings you do not intend. Note also that unless the actors' positions are more or less neutralized or balanced, their very positions in space may give the scene meanings that are not intended.) Use two chairs or a bench.

(*b*) Now play it as on the day after a lovers' quarrel. The man (ONE) is definitely the aggrieved, definitely still very much in love; the woman (TWO) is more or less out-of-love for the moment. With this allocation of lines and roles, play it twice, both times on a park bench. Assume first a bench where they have often met, a bench that is in some ways a symbol of their relationship and of the situation; later assume a bench where they might not have expected to meet at all, a bench unrelated to attendant and preceding circumstances in the situation.

(*c*) Change the roles, but keep the same lines; then keep the same roles but use the other set of lines. Note that the character with lines ONE need not literally ask questions, take the initiative, or pursue a point in the scene, despite certain superficial appearances in the dialogue; but that the character with lines TWO may do these very things. The outer form which the dialogue takes is, as usual, conditioned by the inner motivations.

VII. (*a*) Compose and prepare for presentation before the group four-minute pantomimic exercises — e.g., going through a cafeteria line, passing along one wall of an exhibition. Assume the cafeteria tables or the wall to be downstage, and play the pantomime facing your audience; use no actual properties, but imaginatively handle trays, silver, program, or coat and hat, and the like. In a general way, try to give your pantomime a sense of development and climax. Watch its unity and coherence; keep it simple, though not barren of detail.

(*b*) Under some circumstances, such pantomimes may be used to break the ice before or during a drill or practice session. At other times, and for different but related reasons, the following may be used as ice-breakers: "Up Jenkins" or "Simon says," described in question III, above; nonsense verse, especially when "acted out," or read partly in chorus; tongue-twisters or other articulation exercises; and characterizations or improvisations based on elements that are fantastic or abstract.

VIII. (*a*) Study the Twenty-Third Psalm (page 148) for purposes of reading aloud. Read it to your group, focusing as vividly as possible on communication of its intellectual and emotional content. In this reading, as in later ones, try to avoid stereotyped word groupings or connotations or reactions that may have been carried over from childhood or that may be due to constant repetition and overfamiliarity. At some later time, read it aloud as a prayer of thanksgiving; read it as an individual believer in some higher power, and do not attach its meaning to a specific creed, cosmology, or religious denomination. On another occasion, read it against the background and motivation of a dramatic scene which your group has devised.

(*b*) Read aloud the Mark Twain selection on page 163. How does your consciousness of the hoax or fraud that the author is perpetrating lead you to read the introductory lines of lyrical description? Discuss this point fully with your group. Find another paragraph of superficially similar descriptive material; read both selections aloud and discuss the problem again.

IX. (*a*) Find love scenes, recognition scenes, quarrels, expository scenes, scenes of action, and the like in plays of different form, style, mood, and authorship. Comment specifically on the ways in which playing the scenes must vary according to: the total characterization of the actors involved; the place and function of the scene in the play's entire dramatic action; the theme and style of the whole.

(*b*) Recall and describe to the group scenes from amateur or professional productions in which an actor seemed lost in his character, to the detriment of projection and teamwork. Recall others in which an actor seemed so preoccupied with his "acting" that vividness, smoothness, and naturalness were missing.

X. Prepare and act out selected scenes from Appendix E, pages 173-215, repeating some scenes tried previously, before you had reached this point in the manual. Compare presentations of the same scene by at least two casts. In some cases, let the scene be played by actors generally unfamiliar with the whole manuscript from which the scene has been cut; have these actors repeat the scene after study and analysis of the entire play.

★★★★★★★

7 | Playing the Part

As a final means of strengthening (and, from another point of view, a final means of evaluating) the actor's preparation, several additional suggestions are offered here. For the most part, though not without exception, they are addressed to the actor-as-actor rather than to the actor-as-character, to the interpreter rather than to the impersonator. In accordance with the view established throughout the book, however, and particularly in the last chapter, these suggestions need not be conceived as in any way foreign to the actor's characterization. On the whole, they should be looked upon as ways of heightening expression within character and play, and of adapting the expressiveness of both to the normal requirements of the stage and the theater.

Insuring Clarity

1. *Emphasize any business of especial importance to the plot.* This would include handling the fatal letter, hiding the suspicious handkerchief, discovering the long-lost money, and the like. In a broader sense it would include also the "planting," in pantomime, of ideas that are later to be developed dramatically by the playwright. In all such cases, be sure that the audience sees both object and action, and clearly understands their possible present and future significance.

2. *Similarly, play up the so-called "point" lines — that is, those which every listener must hear and understand if he is to be clear about the progress of the plot.* Examples here are lines telling about situations and character relationships preceding the opening of the play; and lines that foreshadow or

account for something that is to happen later on, or that refer back to important elements in the development of the plot. Be sure also to be absolutely clear in your pronunciation of proper names, so that there can be no confusion as to who did what, or where. Note that plot business and plot lines can be clear without being so distorted as to seem artificial, obtrusive, or distracting. On the other hand, an audience that has missed or only half understood significant bits of exposition may find an entire act vague or pointless.

3. *Start all acts, particularly the first, clearly and deliberately.* Knowing little about the scene and possibly about the character and the plot, the audience needs some time to get its ideas into focus — and, incidentally, to get used to your voice and perhaps your pronunciation. For five or eight minutes after a play begins, and for briefer periods after each intermission, a good actor takes special pains to be heard and understood. Once its attention is caught and its understanding satisfied, an audience will let its interest in your character be fostered and guided as the play proceeds. The fact that some opening scenes are, properly enough, intended to be fast and furious does not invalidate the basic point that I have been trying to establish here.

4. *Check the volume and resonance of your voice and your general projection throughout.* No listener can be clear about what he has not heard or has heard indistinctly. And in plays — unlike lectures, for example — sequences cannot be repeated; an opportunity once lost is lost forever. For this reason, if no other, it is best to rehearse whenever possible in a hall whose size and acoustic properties in general approximate those of the theater which is to be used for performance.

5. *Don't get hidden behind large properties, parts of scenery, or other actors unless the manuscript or your director's design requires it.* Generally speaking, you must be *seen* in order to attract and hold attention; and this means being seen from practically any seat in the house. However, do not suppress naturalness by hesitating to play close to ordinary furniture, or to touch it, stand against it, and the like. The present

rule applies to gross bodily attitudes and action as well as to minor gestures and movement. Try not to hide or bury gestures or business behind your own or another actor's body, or behind various parts of the setting. A brilliantly conceived, accurately presented, and richly motivated action of any kind is lost on an audience that has failed to see and comprehend it.

6. *In general, develop and show a sense of "geography" in relation to objects or places mentioned in the play.* A gesture of the hand, a nod of the head, or merely a glance toward some point (on or off stage) helps to emphasize its importance and significance as it is brought up from time to time in the dialogue. If the actor's *attitude* is right, a simple and unobtrusive movement is usually sufficient. The inexperienced or insensitive actor sometimes treats what has happened, or is happening, "upstairs" or "just outside the window" as though it had happened somewhere else or as though it had no relation to what he was saying or doing at the moment. On a somewhat different level, he sometimes refers to a kitchen, a living room, or a front hall as though its architectural relation to the setting had changed several times during the course of the action, as though he had no clear notion about the rest of the house and no particular interest in it. Unless such vagueness is in point (as with a stranger whose ignorance of the situation may have dramatic value), it is likely to be utterly confusing to an audience.

7. *Be careful to avoid all distracting attitudes, postures, movements, and gestures.* Many scenes are not clear to the spectator simply because his attention has been drawn to awkward, irrelevant, or overcomplicated action at moments when he should have been listening or looking for something else. The distraction may be due to a superficially conceived and improperly motivated characterization, to inadequate rehearsal of difficult or unfamiliar routines, to overplaying, or to a combination of these and other factors. The net effect is the same in each case: the audience misses a point and must assimilate the scene's meaning without it.

8. *Be consistent.* Avoid dullness and monotony, but stay in

character; and stay in *your* character. Every moment you are on the stage, even when you appear to be doing nothing, you are in a positive or negative way affecting the total impression that your part is making on the audience. A barren and obvious simplicity is monotonous, it is true; but extreme complexity or multiplicity of stimuli is merely confusing and unclear. If the audience is to understand your character, it must be able to assimilate the character's varied appearances and manifestations into a single unified whole.

9. *Watch the ensemble effect throughout.* Play to and with the others; keep to the director's over-all design. It is no virtue to have dwarfed a major scene or a major character by highlighting a minor one. When you throw off the balance or proportion of the production as a whole, you distort its values and its meanings.

Insuring Interest

1. *Keep the dialogue moving, even at the expense — if absolutely necessary — of characterization and naturalness.* Cut in on the ends of previous lines whenever you can do so without destroying the point. If you cannot naturally begin your line until the last word of the earlier one has been spoken, remember that you can usually begin to register a reaction and *prepare* to speak before that time. This does not mean rushing and jumbling together the first words of your speech; it does mean starting your speech, or the entire reaction pattern, as early as possible. Starting promptly and speaking rapidly are two different and not necessarily related things: your character can react promptly to cue and yet speak and move with the utmost deliberation. A typical contemporary play may have as many as twelve or fifteen hundred separate cues. If a second or even a fraction of a second is lost between cues, the actors have added from ten to twenty or twenty-five minutes to the playing time; and what is worse, they have so distracted the audience's attention and dulled its interest that the performance has seemed even longer and flatter than it has actually been.

Two characters from Paul Green's THE HOUSE OF
CONNELLY.   Carnegie Institute of Technology.

Leonora confronts the sisters, in Percy and Denham's
LADIES IN RETIREMENT.   Cornell University Theatre.

The action at a climax in THE INSPECTOR GENERAL.
University of Minnesota Theatre.

From the Epilogue to R.U.R., by Karl Capek,
as presented at Cornell University.

2. *Keep the dialogue varied.* Watch for every possible opportunity to change the tempo, the pitch, or the general flavor of your line-reading in accordance with the demands of the manuscript; be sensitive to every nuance of character and interpretation that will vary your delivery within the normal limits of over-all unity and consistency. Remember also that properly motivated and controlled pauses can add to the interest as well as the meaning of your readings. Concentrate at the moment of delivery; be aware of, and respond freely to, every contrast in meaning, mood, or attitude. Don't hurry; take time to react. If repetition and familiarity have dulled your responsivness, set out at once to restore the correctness and the vividness of your impressions and reactions.

3. *Suppress any tendency to imitate other actors in pitch, tempo, volume, and the like.* Never — consciously or unconsciously — take your "tone" or "level" from the other fellow. If he is acting his part and you are acting yours, the chances are that the differences between you are far more important than the similarities. Remember to play up these differences, and avoid the much-too-easy habit of unconscious imitation. That most of the other characters in a given scene are relatively loud or strident, or that they are relatively slow and deliberate, is in itself certainly no indication that your cues for speech and behavior should be identical with theirs. To obscure the natural differences between you and the others may not only weaken the vitality of the scene, but may distort your characterization and misrepresent its relation to the structure of the play.

4. *In the same way, play up the differences between scenes.* With every new scene, the entrance of new characters, the reporting or discovery of new information, the establishment of new dramatic desires, show a clear and decided *change.* Your part and the director's design may demand that you change your tempo, your spirit, your volume, your position, or all of these. But change! If contrasts in general — and such items as plot reversals in particular — are missed or are badly handled, your production will seem to run down hill; to get

less rather than more interesting as the action proceeds. The play itself is changing, growing, developing. The actors must be certain to project its inherent variety.

5. *Play up the high spots within the individual scenes and the big scene within the play as a whole.* Watch for climaxes, both major and minor, and be sure to work gradually but insistently toward them. Never pass them by at the same pace and on the same level that you used for the scenes which preceded them. Within the limits set by naturalness and by genuine motivation, make the dramatic spots dramatic. In a good production, this does not of course automatically mean clenched fists, raucous screams, and melodramatic attitudes; it may mean tense quiet and utter simplicity. But much of a production's strength and vitality normally lies in its emotional crescendo, its cumulative effect. The play's highlights must be accented, not shadowed by minor scenes or minor characters; and the play's main climax must to some degree and in some sense top all that has gone before.

6. *Learn to conserve as well as to build.* Don't throw all your physical and nervous energy into your performance in the earlier scenes. If you have used up your reserves in Act I, your later efforts to accent a climax may betray the strain under which you are working. Even if, as in some plays, an early scene is emotionally intense, you will still need to keep the end in view as you decide on the emotional level at which you can pitch the scene; and you will need to start thereafter — if possible, at a new and lower level of intensity — a gradual build toward the climaxes that are to come. In any case, a sledgehammer attack at the very beginning may be merely confusing to an audience. Remember that an audience is cold at the start, is without intellectual and emotional orientation; and that you must usually establish contact on a relatively low level of intensity and then take the audience with you, so to speak, thereafter.

7. *Don't move too often in a short scene, nor too seldom in a long one.* If there are too many calls on a spectator's attention over a short period of time, he finds it difficult to focus on

any one of them and so loses interest in all. Conversely, if his interest is not attracted visually at several critical points in a long scene, he may find the dialogue talky and dull. But remember the warning that has been frequently repeated throughout the manual: guard against restless, irrelevant, or unmotivated action at any time.

8. *Wait for, but don't wait out, the laughs.* Don't rush ahead with the dialogue when your audience has an opportunity and a desire to laugh. The audience will be annoyed at your suppression of its appreciation, as well as disconcerted by the fact that it has missed some of the lines. If you wait too long, however (that is to say, beyond the point where the laugh has really begun to die down), you will tend to slow up the play and break its continuity. In some cases your director may plan to kill a few successive small laughs in order to build for a bigger one later; but these are some of the proverbial exceptions that prove the rule. Holding for laughs is in most cases imperative, and it usually requires all the concentration, all the skill, and all the insight that you can muster.

9. *Above all, be clear.* Clearness may be possible without interest, but interest is inconceivable without clarity. An audience can rarely work up an interest in what it does not understand.

Checking Up On The Whole

1. *Has your performance been sufficiently VARIED throughout?* In ordinary circumstances, monotony can do more to ruin the success of your production than can any other single item. Monotony is the foe of expressiveness — and, so far as your audience is concerned, it is the foe of attention. Holding attention usually means recapturing attention. The interest of your spectators must constantly be revived by a succession of new and fresh appeals. Variety, as the old adage has it, is the spice of life; certainly variety is the spice of the theater.

2. *Has your performance been sufficiently BRISK?* This implies an intelligent alertness as to picking up cues, reacting to

changes and contrasts, and keeping the action moving in general. Conversely, of course, it implies knowing when to take *more* time rather than less, as a particular scene or bit of business may require. But remember that on the whole it is better to play too rapidly than too slowly. Never, in short, let your scenes drag.

3. *Has your performance been accomplished WITHOUT STRAIN?* Note that a good performance never suggests that an actor is working too hard. His most important actions are performed and his most telling lines are delivered without apparent strain, so that the audience is unconscious of the effort involved. Any vocal or pantomimic effect that seems forced should be modified, if not suppressed, in rehearsal. In performance, let your work seem restrained, effortless, easy.

A Primer of Stage Directing

FOR THE BEGINNING ACTOR

As its title and its content thus far suggest, this manual is about acting rather than about directing or any other phase of dramatic production. On the other hand, although the actor's and the director's functions should not be confused, the two functions do have so much in common and do overlap at so many points that at times it is almost impossible to speak of one without including the other. For this reason — and because the beginning actor can usually work more intelligently and more effectively when he knows what the director is doing and why — it has seemed advisable to append here certain elementary material which is usually the concern of a director but is of interest and value to the actor as well.

In its simplest terms, the director's task is to translate into theatrical language the form, purpose, and meaning of a playwright's manuscript. His principal medium of expression is the actor — the actor's voice and body, the actor's movements in space and time, the actor's physical and psychological relations to the setting and to the other actors. To this medium the director adds others perhaps less important, including the setting itself, light, costume, make-up, and so on, and their interrelationships. Primarily, the director is an artist, though almost inevitably he is an executive as well; and, particularly in the non-professional theater, he is likely to be a teacher also, even though his work does not happen to be connected with a school or college program. The present section is intended as a brief account of some aspects of a director's function as an artist.

The student has been advised from time to time to consider the director's *design*. This we may define as a selective arrangement of expressive details by which he projects a unified and coherent artistic message to an audience. It is in the nature of art in general and of theatrical art in particular that the individual actor's design must be assimilated into the director's larger one, if there is to be singleness of communicative purpose and effect. The actor interprets or creates (depending in large part on a definition of terms) within the larger plan, giving it vitality and concreteness but not destroying its unity or proportion. It is best not to look upon the director's over-all scheme as tyrannical or inhibitory. Just as an actor must work within the form of the author's manuscript (including its stage directions and its general prescriptions, implied or explicit, as to speech and movement), so he must work within the director's form, including its directions and prescriptions.

To take only the single example of directions for basic physical movements: many more productions, both amateur and professional, have been handicapped by restless and ambiguous movement on the part of the actors than by controlled and designed movement imposed by the director. Many more productions have been handicapped by lack of purpose and unity in the broad patterns of action and space relations than by the imposition of such patterns by a director. John Dolman has, as usual, been both lucid and reasonable on this point. In commenting on a passage from Harley Granville-Barker's *The Exemplary Theatre,* Professor Dolman writes (the italics are mine):

> There is positively only one way in which a good actor, in anything but a highly declamatory play, can avoid agitating his mind about physical movements at an actual performance, and that is by having them so well learned in advance that he can perform them without agitation; *only thus can he purchase the real freedom of mind necessary to real freedom of interpretation.*[1]

[1] *The Art of Play Production* (Harpers, rev. ed., 1946), pp. 100-101.

Professor Dolman is of course referring to basic patterns of movement included in the director's blocking out of the action. If, he continues, a specific movement planned by the director later proves inconsistent with the development of an actor's interpretation, there is obviously a legitimate and proper reason for change. The conscientious director will go to almost any lengths to avoid methods or directions that may inhibit the actor, make his performance mechanical, or check his creative impulses. But the director is after all the one who is responsible for the production as a whole — is, indeed, the only one who can "see" the production as a whole. In supplying fundamental patterns of movement, the director is trying to avoid awkward or misleading stage pictures; to suppress clumsy or irrelevant movements that may seem to be working at cross-purposes with other movements; and in general to guide and control actors who get in each other's way, blanket each other's lines, and play important bits from unemphatic positions.

In conceiving and executing his over-all design, your director is guided by such elements as unity, proportion, balance, and rhythm. Common to all the arts, and to all phases of dramatic production, these design elements are of concern also to the actor. The first of them, *unity*, that is to say, singleness of purpose, meaning, arrangement, or effect, is historically as well as experimentally established as a basic principle of beauty. Indeed, it is recognized by most schools of psychology as a basic principle of perception. The human mind and body tend to perceive an object or a phenomenon as a unity, as a relation between more or less harmonious parts making up a single whole. Where unity is not immediately or ultimately apparent, we tend to search for it. Having achieved it, we find pleasure as well as meaning in the unification; having failed to achieve it, we are restless, confused, or dissatisfied.

Thus, we tend to discover a unity in almost any multiplicity of objects — stars, spots on a paper, pieces of furniture, groups of persons, sounds repeated in time, the separate parts of a natural or artificial arrangement of any kind. We sometimes achieve unification of the parts as merely numerical units in time or space; on other occasions we find relations between their various characteristics or attributes. On higher levels we find in the several parts of a whole a unity of thought or purpose or spirit, and we say that some objects possess unity of (and between) form and content. When too many unrelated or loosely related items are placed in a still life, a sculpture, a stage picture, or the reading of a line, we cannot perceive it as a unity, and we are bewildered as to its meaning as well as dissatisfied with its effect. Similarly, when unrelated forms, moods, styles, or ideas are placed crudely in juxtaposition, we get an aesthetic jar or shock.

Your director is aware of the unification principle at many points and on various levels in his work — from the casting of his actors to the selection and arrangement of curtains on his set, from the grouping of his actors to the timing and tone-coloration of the play's separate scenes. He bears it in mind as he correlates sound with sound, voice with voice, speech with speech, and all with action; and as he adapts the entire pattern to values in time as well as in space. But he recognizes, as must his actors, that the unity he arrives at must not be too simple or obvious, lest it be monotonous and only momentarily interesting. Within its unity, an understandable and satisfying object must display variety — of number, kind, attribute, or arrangement. Sustained interest usually demands singleness in multiplicity and complexity, unity in variety. If the phenomenon is too varied, it cannot be grasped and is unsatisfying; if it is too simple, it is likely to be dull and without continuing interest.

The principle of unification apparently exerts an influence on, and may be basic to, other design elements. *Proportion* (which we usually associate with *relationships* of *size, quantity, or degree*) may, for example, be explained in part by its kinship with unity-in-variety. Every time two lines or shapes, two parts of any whole, are placed side by side, proportions are established which may be good or bad, pleasing or unsatisfactory, unifying or divisive. If we divide a line or shape exactly in half, as at A in Figure I, the resulting proportions, while not downright unpleasant, are still monotonous, obvious, and uninteresting. There is too much equality or sameness. If on the other hand we divide a line or shape too far from the middle (as at B in Figure I), the disproportion is somewhat annoying and distracting, since the two parts vary so greatly as to seem unrelated; here there is too much inequality or variety. The proportions illustrated at C in Figure I are on the whole most interesting and satisfying, and can be supported as such by a certain amount of experimental evidence.

The 60:40 arrangement in Figure I, C (and in the topmost area in Figure II) displays the so-called Greek proportions. Traditionally these are accepted as more attractive and satisfying than proportions depending either on approximately equal divisions of line, space, or mass or on strongly conflicting divisions. Most volumes on psychology and aesthetics call attention also to the so-called golden section. This represents a proportion in which the smaller of two divisions bears the same relation to the larger division as the larger does to the whole. Mathematically, the ratio involved in the golden sec-

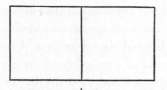 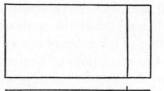

A. Approximately 50:50   B. Approximately 85:15

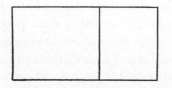

C. Approximately 60:40

Figure I. Lines and areas divided in varying **proportions**.

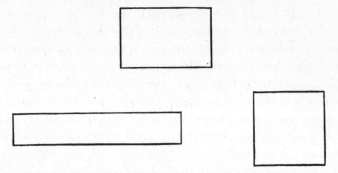

Figure II. **Areas with dimensions of varying proportions.** The area is the same in each of the three cases, but is shaped by length-and-breadth proportions of 85:15, 60:40, and 50:50.

tion (approximately 62 to 38) is not markedly different from the Greek ratio, mentioned above (3 to 2, or 60 to 40). Expressed as a formula, the golden section becomes: x : y :: y : x + y; or, very roughly, 5 : 8 :: 8 : 13.

Your director applies his knowledge of, and feeling for, proportion in various ways during production. The illustrations used above have for the sake of simplicity and clarity been visual ones; but the principle which they illustrate carries over into the realm of the auditory as well as of the visual, and into that of the subjective as well as of the objective. Exaggerations or distortions of character, and over-playing in general, are fundamentally matters of proportion. So is the relative strength of the highlights that an actor gives to a minor character or a minor scene, at the expense of major ones. Decisions — both theoretical and practical — as between theme and plot, characterization and atmosphere, lines and business, or thought and emotion, are other such problems.

In all of these, as in purely visual composition, there need be nothing dogmatic about applications of the Greek or golden ratios or of any other factor in proportion, which after all can be only approximate guides. In dividing a line or shape, the critical point need not be located mechanically, since any division approximating 3:2 proportions is relatively and potentially pleasing; and in any case to follow the same procedure always would result in monotony and sterility. Moreover, in a complicated pattern, there may well be individual units of less pleasing proportions, although the proportions of the whole and the interrelation of parts may be meaningful and satisfying. The point to be stressed is again unity-in-variety. As before, the ideal is neither oversimplified and possibly monotonous unity, nor overcomplicated variety in which the parts may be too difficult to relate easily one to the other.

Balance (i.e., of weights, interests, or forces) is closely related to proportion as the latter has just been presented. The simplest form of balance, represented by weights on a teeter-totter, is easily recognized. Schoolboys of equal weight are in balance so long as they are the same distance from the center; a heavier boy must move toward the center or a lighter one away from the center if they are to stay in balance. In the arts, however, balance is not so much a question of actual weight as of apparent or psychological weight — of *attention-value* weight. If your director were to put the two boys of equal weight on the stage, one in a bright red sweater, the other in a dull brown one, then in balancing them against a common background he would have to move the red-sweatered one appreciably closer to the center than the other.

Beyond color and color intensity, there are on the stage such factors to consider as apparent weight or size, light and shadow, silence and sound, and immobility as opposed to real or suggested movement. There is also the established psychological importance or dramatic value of one character in relation to others. No two persons or objects, or groups of these, can be treated in the theater as though they were metal weights on a balance scale.

Moreover, your director is not always concerned on the stage with formal (or "obvious") balance. Depending on the nature and style of the play or the scene, he may wish to establish more or less formal balance, and even on occasion perfect symmetry. Such an arrangement — achieved physically or psychologically — may afford the quiet dignity, the sense of order, or the simple balance of forces which the situation demands. Usually, however, perfect symmetry is too mechanical and uninteresting for use on the stage. More frequently the director aims at informal (or "occult") balance, which is more subtle, more varied, and ordinarily more interesting. Here again the basic principle of unity-in-variety, of just-so-far but not-too-far (in this case, from perfect symmetry), comes into play.

Rhythm is an over-used, and doubtless much-abused, word. To some writers and speakers it seems to mean inner tempo, characteristic trait or motivation, inherent mood or atmosphere, and much else that is sometimes vague and often confusing to the beginner. But rhythm so pervades all artistic expression and is so important to all artistic effort that the beginning actor is obligated to face and if possible resolve the difficulty of language. His insight into the meaning of the word and into its various aesthetic manifestations will doubtless grow with his experience, but in the meantime he needs to find a basic meaning that will serve him as a frame of reference.

As it is commonly understood, rhythm is concerned with movement — movement in time or space; in sound, line, mass, or color; in subjective or objective details or units. Its distinguishing characteristic is a more or less regular (though not necessarily simple) recurrence of elements of one kind or another; and the recurrence is of such a nature that it can be perceived, consciously or unconsciously, as organized and progressive. The painter may achieve controlled and rhythmic movement by a subtle repetition of line or mass, or by a progression of sizes, shapes, or colors. Patterns of recurrent stress in music are on some levels more obvious than those in painting, and may be more widely recognized. The poet's rhythms are traditionally more formal and often more simple and direct than the prose writer's, though rhythmical patterns are clearly marked in some types of prose. Wherever in the arts there is a recurrence of, or alternation in, tempo, stress, coloration, light or shadow, physical or psychological action, there is potentially some type of rhythm.

The rhythms in expressionistic or other non-conventional plays are likely to be bold and inescapable; and in projecting them to an audience your director will need your understanding and co-operation. He will need them far more frequently, however, and in far more subtle ways for conventional productions. He may see possibilities for rhythmical arrangement in the composition of his stage pictures, or of his sound-patterns within a given scene. He may wish to echo situation with situation, conflict with conflict, desire with desire. He may play character against character or scene against scene with a recurrent accent of tempo, volume, pitch, or mood.

The rhythm which you must recognize and help to project may be exceedingly simple, as in *leisurely to FAST to leisurely to FAST;* or in *light to light to DARK to light to light to DARK.* It may be somewhat more complex, as in *boisterous to SERENE to stormy to SERENE to gay to SERENE to tragic to SERENE.* It may be concerned with the pitch of a voice or the position of a body in space. It may be concerned with the play's plot structure — e.g., desire, *frustration,* desire, *frustration,* desire, *frustration,* DEFEAT. As with other design elements, the pattern may be so simple as to be uninteresting, so crude as to call attention to itself, or so imperfect or difficult to assimilate as to leave an audience bewildered and unsatisfied.

Apart from the design elements [2] examined so far, your director is aware also of another, which is somewhat different though not unrelated: *emphasis.* Here he is concerned with (1) the intensity of the impression which his entire design makes on the beholder, and (2) the relative value or importance which the design ascribes to various parts of the whole. Within his design, the director must focus on a single center

[2] For more detailed treatments of unity, proportion, balance, and rhythm, the student may wish to consult such volumes as Dolman's *The Art of Play Production,* already cited, or Samuel Selden, *The Stage in Action* (Crofts, 1941). Herbert Sidney Langfeld, *The Aesthetic Attitude* (Harcourt, Brace, 1920) and Robert Morris Ogden, *The Psychology of Art* (Scribner's, 1938), though not devoted primarily to design in the theater, are of special interest to the director and the actor.

of interest (i.e., the *right* center of interest), and must focus on other details in the order of their importance to his purpose at the moment. Since on the stage there is such a complexity of stimuli in light, color, mass, sound, and movement, and since that very complexity is usually shifting or moving, the director faces in the broad area of "emphasis" some of his most crucial decisions.

Your director has doubtless gained some of his experience in handling problems of emphasis from his observation of painting and the other arts. There he has observed, for example, that intensities should be relative, that if everything is vivid nothing is vivid. He has taken notes on the placing or grouping of objects and of their relation to a background; he has recognized the emphatic effect of the unusual or the unexpected. He has probably combined these observations with his knowledge of experimental science. The psychology of attention, for instance, is of primary importance in his work, as it must ultimately be in your own.

Though an audience can attend to almost anything that is made sufficiently interesting, it is clear that some types of stimuli make stronger demands on attention than do others. To put it another way, certain characteristics or values [3] present in most stimuli are more emphatic than others. *Strength* or *intensity* of stimulus (comparative vividness, loudness, or brightness, and in some cases size or amount) is of course one such value. Another is its *duration,* or the insistence with which it is repeated. Still a third is *movement* or *velocity,* actual or suggested. A fourth attention value is *definiteness of form,* which has been discussed earlier in another connection; the sharply defined, in time or in space, always attracts more attention than the vague or the disorganized.

A fifth value, *variety* or *change,* is of importance not only in itself but in its relation to the other values. That is to say, a sustained or repeated stimulus, attractive at first, may cease in

[3] Professor Woodworth has used the term "factors of advantage" in attention. See Robert S. Woodworth, *Psychology,* rev. ed. (Holt, 1934), chapter IX; also Jon Eisenson, *The Psychology of Speech* (Crofts, 1938), chapter XIV.

time to attract notice; and silence or inaction against a background of sound or movement is bound to call attention to itself. Changes or contrasts within any of the values are attention-catching, *per se*. Then, too, there are additional attention values not dependent solely on the nature of the object or stimulus presented on the stage at any given moment. Just how and to what a spectator will pay attention is of course conditioned also by his previous experience and by his personal desires or interests at the time. If he is too hot or otherwise uncomfortable or distracted by conditions in the house — or if he has missed certain details of exposition or orientation that should have been "planted" in his consciousness earlier in the performance — he may find it difficult to attend to a scene on the stage, no matter how clear or vivid the scene may be momentarily. The cause of the difficulty or failure in a scene during the second act may thus not lie within the scene itself, but may be attributable to the shortcomings of an earlier scene or scenes.

So much for attention values in general, as they apply in part to theatrical production. The space arrangements on a typical stage and their relation to the space arrangements in a typical auditorium are worthy of special mention. As Figure III A suggests, the onstage space within an average setting can be arbitrarily divided into six areas. The sightlines imposed on that space in Figure III B indicate one reason why the UR and UL areas are ordinarily weaker in their attention value and in their general usefulness for important action. For most spectators, a greater effort is required to see objects or actions UL or UR than to see them elsewhere, if indeed they can in some cases see them in those areas at all. For this reason and for other aesthetic or psychological ones, the stage areas are usually listed as follows in order of their normal attention value:

Strongest:	down center
Stronger:	up center
Strong:	down right and down left
Weak:	up right and up left

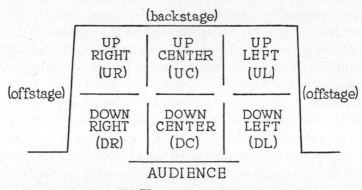

A. The stage areas

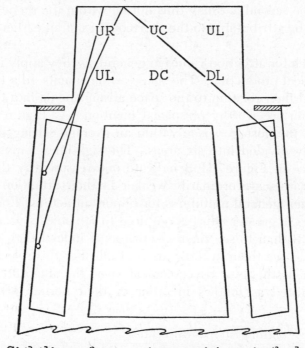

B. Sightlines from various positions in the house

Figure III.

Two warnings are necessary in connection with this list: first, "strong" and "weak" as applied here are relative terms. If only one actor or a pair of actors appears on the stage, the strongest position may be DC, as suggested in the list. If, however, other actors DL and DR focus on the original pair, and if the entire stage picture now approximates a triangle whose base is down stage and whose apex is up stage, then the original pair may well be strongest UC rather than DC. Similarly, levels raised from the stage floor, brightly lighted areas, and other factors may temporarily rearrange the values as they appear on the list.

A second warning is that "strong" and "weak" are not to be conceived of as necessarily the equivalent of "good" or "bad," "right" or "wrong," "effective" or "ineffective," in any particular case. For some characters in some circumstances, a weak area or position is obviously the good, the right, and the effective one.

Within the areas, or in the playing space as a whole, advancing movements are normally stronger than retreating ones — movements down stage or toward center, or from sitting to standing positions, stronger than their opposites. Here again values are relative. Naturally the physical nature and the psychological weight of a movement affects its relative strength as much as does the movement's direction in space; and what is going on elsewhere, visually or audibly, may affect its relative strength even more. An audience does attend to sound rather than silence, to sight rather than sound, to the living rather than the inanimate, to the moving rather than the inactive, to the unusual or unexpected rather than the commonplace. But conditions on the stage are so fluid and values on the stage are so relative that it is unwise to be dogmatic or mechanical. Whenever you have an impulse to be arbitrary about the strength of an area, a position, or a movement, check yourself with questions like the following: On what stage? In what set; during what scene; in what play; under what conditions?

Out of such facts, such principles, and such relative values as these, then, your director creates his design for your production. Into this language he translates his view of the play's essential meaning. His task, and yours, is at once larger and more difficult than this brief and partial summary can have indicated. But in so far as this summary has helped to broaden your understanding of the common task, and in so far as it has helped to bring other parts of the manual into manageable focus, it can serve as a useful section of your basic training.

A Primer of
Theater Aesthetics

FOR THE BEGINNING ACTOR

Throughout most of Appendix A, and elsewhere in the manual, the student has been dealing with facts, principles, and judgments that could be broadly considered as "aesthetic." Almost everywhere in the book he has been urged to consider artistic purpose and effect, to focus on designed selection and arrangement of details, and to be aware of an audience more or less intent on viewing an object of art. The present section summarizes certain of these considerations, introduces new and relevant material, and applies both to dramatic production as a whole.

The art of the theater, as it is conceived in our time, is non-imitative or anti-imitative. Even in so-called naturalistic productions, neither the setting nor the acting is intended to photograph, reproduce, or imitate life as it is known outside the theater. If a theatrical production mirrors actuality in any sense, the accent is on the mirroring and not on the actuality; artistic selection, conventionalization, and idealization are avowedly at work. Any "illusion" which the spectator is asked to accept is predicated — to borrow a familiar phrase — on a willing suspension of disbelief and not on any delusion or deception as to actual "reality."

Accordingly, then, the theater artist must take special pains to control the spectator's *attitude* as well as his attention, to control the frame of mind and spirit in which he approaches and accepts the production. The aesthetic attitude has been variously described; [1] perhaps "detached and disinterested contemplation" will serve best for present purposes. The basic fact is that a spectator with the desired attitude reacts *in* the dramatic situation, so to speak, rather than *to* the situation; and he is not disposed to do anything about it in a real-life sense, interrupt it, own it, change or control it, take part in it. However, although he does remain detached and disinterested, he is vitally alive to its independent, imaginative, non-actual "reality."

To put the problem in another way, the theater artist must take special pains to establish and maintain conditions favorable to aesthetic "distance." Somewhat as the sculptor places his statue on a pedestal and the painter encloses his painting in a frame to set them off from the actuality of their surroundings, the artist of the theater normally raises his typical productions up on a stage, keeps them in a sense behind a curtained frame, and dims down the auditorium lights as the curtain is drawn. The term *distance* is of course relative and more or less figurative; it is as much psychological as physical, and it refers as much to an attitude within the spectator as it does to the spectator's actual position in space. Even in specialized productions in which the actor breaks through the frame and in a sense addresses the spectator directly (of which more in a moment), he carefully fosters a certain kind of distance lest the spectator misunderstand him and take him for something he is not. In short, theater art must be neither so "real" that it deludes or deceives the spectator, nor so "close" (physically or psychologically) that it jars him out of his imaginative illusion and brings him back to an actual world, with its everyday values, desires, and frustrations.

The exact nature and source of a spectator's aesthetic pleasure are matters about which we can only speculate. One of the most interesting and possibly most useful theories in this connection is concerned with motor responses which, it is as-

[1] See, for example, Langfeld, *op. cit.*, chapter III; and Alexander Bakshy, *The Theatre Unbound* (Cecil Palmer, London, 1923), chapter V. A useful anthology of modern aesthetic theories, including a brief critical summary, is: Melvin M. Rader, *A Modern Book of Esthetics* (Holt, 1935).

sumed, are set up within the spectator. At times, the motor responses show outwardly; more frequently they are experienced unconsciously and inwardly as merely motor sets or attitudes, or relatively weak imitative impulses. In either case, the muscular set or attitude is assumed to condition, if not to cause, the spectator's perception of such experiences as weight, form, smoothness, grace, and the like. In a process now widely known as "empathy"[2] the motor and other adjustments which the spectator makes within his own body are projected into the object he is observing, and seem to be a part or characteristic of the object itself. Broadly speaking, the spectator imaginatively projects his consciousness into persons on the stage, imaginatively identifies himself with theatrical objects or situations.

For example, the grace of a line or the fitness of a character's motivation seems to be an attribute of the line or the motivation. Actually, the source of the spectator's pleasure or satisfaction lies in the ease of his adjustment to the line or the motivation. According to the theory of empathy, the perception of such qualities as grace or fitness is dependent solely on neither the object nor the observer, *per se*, but on the *relation* between the two. That is to say, the nature of a motor response or adjustment depends on two factors and their interrelationship: (1) the nature of the object observed; (2) the nature of the past experience and present attitude of the observer. The theory thus allows for intellectual as well as purely sensuous elements in art and the theater; and allows for "objects" that exist in time and in space, in sound and in sight, in memory and imagination as well as in the physical world.

In cases where we can apply the theory of empathy, we may then have one more explanation for — or, at least, one more manifestation of — a breakdown in the aesthetic attitude. If a spectator's empathic adjustment is too difficult, or if a series of empathic adjustments are too difficult to unify, he is aware of confusion and dissatisfaction; and he may begin to think of

<hr>

[2] So translated by Titchener from Lipps. For a detailed discussion see Langfeld, *op. cit.*, especially chapters V and VI, and Rader, *op. cit.*, chapter VIII.

something else, or to observe the object other than aesthetically.

In any event, we have so far established one basic distinction of importance to the theater artist: between an aesthetic world or reality and an actual world or reality; between a world of which a spectator is a detached and disinterested observer and a world in which he is a dynamically interested participant. But within the aesthetic world of the theater there are levels or degrees, as it were, of audience participation. Since the form and style in which plays are conceived differ somewhat in this respect, the degrees or levels of difference are worthy of examination. Fundamental in any distinction between plays and between productions are the major divisions of *illusionistic* and *non-illusionistic*. Most of the plays mounted in the contemporary theater (indeed, most of the plays written since Ibsen) are illusionistic in purpose. Conceived of as creating an effect of theatrical reality more or less independent of an audience, these plays are stage-centered. The audience is by no means forgotten, but it is not directly recognized and it is not required to participate in any obvious way. In general, the actor-as-character takes precedence over the actor-as-actor, and there is no direct communication between actor and audience. Alexander Bakshy has called the illusionistic type *representational,* and has designated the non-illusionistic, audience-centered type as *presentational.*

Most plays written before Ibsen, and some written since, are fundamentally presentational or non-illusionistic. Addressed more or less directly to an audience, they attempt to create no theatrical illusion of reality; they frankly "present" a dramatic action or spectacle, rather than "represent" an image of life that may seem to exist at times independent of the theater. They may be written in more or less formal language, even in blank verse; and they may have been played originally on a platform which — though it projected out into the seating space and was without stage decoration as the modern theater understands it — was meant to indicate a battlefield, a street, a temple, or a dwelling place. In these plays the actor-as-actor predominates over the actor-as-character, and may address the audience directly as chorus or narrator, or in asides or soliloquies. It is more obvious throughout the performance that the stage is a stage, the actor an actor, and the theater a theater than is possible or desirable with illusionistic plays. Greek tragedy, Elizabethan and Restoration plays, the comedy of Molière, and such oriental adaptations as *Lady Precious Stream* and *The Yellow Jacket* are essentially presentational, as are the expressionistic plays of the nineteen-twenties and nineteen-thirties.

The observant student may have noticed that so far the term *realistic* has not been used in the present discussion. The omission has been purposeful, inasmuch as illusionistic is sometimes confusing when considered synonymous with realistic; and in as much as the latter term is useful as applied to one separate class of illusionistic plays. That is to say, many, but not all, illusionistic plays are realistic in style; some are *non-realistic* or *fantastic*.[3]

Thus, Lord Dunsany's *Gods of the Mountain* and *The Tents of the Arabs*, although they are illusionistic or representational, do not represent an image of life in terms of the externals of ordinary existence, as do *Ghosts, Escape,* and *The Silver Cord*. Non-realistic plays like Dunsany's are cast in representational form, but do not suggest the patterns of everyday speech and behavior and are not intended to take place in a realistic setting characteristic of other representational plays. The student should note also that *symbolic* is not synonymous with any of the terms used up to this point. Symbolism is common to both non-realistic and realistic plays, and to presentational as well as representational ones.

The elementary but fundamental distinctions here set forth

[3] Professor Hewitt has made this distinction in these terms (*op. cit.,* page 67). In general, his discussion of literary, aesthetic, and structural types brings order and clarity to an array of terms often bewildering to a beginner. As he writes (page 65), some of the terms widely used in recent years apply "to the structure of plays, some to their content, and some to fashions in production which have little to do with essential dramatic forms"; yet the terms are often used indiscriminately and at times synonymously.

carry clear implications for the student of acting. The actor's task is the same for every play — to assimilate and project the playwright's meaning. But his execution of the task must be conditioned by the form and style inherent in any given manuscript. In some productions he must master non-realistic movement and dialogue, both of which may be relatively unfamiliar to him and to a typical audience. In others, he must use realistic conventions, take part in realistic situations and actions, and represent characters realistically conceived. In some he must literally stay within a representational setting, framed by teaser and tormentors behind a proscenium arch; in others he must reach out, physically and psychologically, toward his audience.

In illusionistic productions, the actor must seem to be unaware of his audience, must appear to be unconscious of projecting his voice and his movement, although he has concentrated throughout rehearsals on those very things. In the presentational style, acting is more frankly acting, and the actor's relations with his audience are less subtle and more direct. The audience still believes in the dramatic action, aesthetically and imaginatively; but it is in more obvious ways aware that it is observing a show and not an image of actuality. The audience is conscious of and willing to accept a direct and frank theatricality, unhampered by illusionistic conventions.

The student should recognize that presentationalism and representationalism are relative values, and that neither exists absolutely free of the other. Since plays like *Ghosts* and *Escape* and *The Silver Cord*, although illusionistic in tendency, are conceived and mounted in our time as non-imitative, they therefore retain basic elements of a show in a theater; and to this degree they are partly presentational. On the other hand, there are traces of illusionistic elements in the presentational plays of the past — in Euripides, Shakespeare, Molière. In much of their action and characterization and even in their audience-relationship, there may be recognizable signs of a representational attitude or approach. In Thornton Wilder's *Our Town*, as in his shorter pieces like *Happy Journey* and

Pullman Car Hiawatha, the acting required in some of the
scenes is certainly representational in conception, although
the play's frank treatment of the stage as an acting place and
of the narrator as a direct communicator with the audience are
clearly presentational.

The point is that one play or production may be predominantly representational, another predominantly presentational; but each must stay within aesthetic (i.e., non-actual)
bounds. There are degrees of audience recognition from the
stage, and in a sense degrees of audience participation from
the auditorium. But there are extremes at either end, and
actual audience participation at either extreme is in the contemporary view non-aesthetic.

At one extreme is an imitative, stage-centered naturalism
that may deceive an audience and encourage real participation
— i.e., encourage an impulse to interrupt a play, to join in literally with its action, or to view it in any way except in detached
and disinterested contemplation. At the other extreme is an
audience-centered naturalism that may have gone beyond
frank theatricality and may have encouraged real participation
on the part of some spectators.[4] A presentational actor who is
close to a spectator is in some respects more real than a representational one who is far enough away. An actor may represent a character behind the proscenium frame, or he may present a character from an apron or forestage; in neither case
must he be mistaken for anything but an actor. Horror or suffering may be acted presentationally or representationally in
the theater (and may be tragic, comic, or farcical in its purpose and effect), but in no case must it be mistaken for actuality.

The broad divisions here set forth offer a basic scheme for

[4] A special kind of example here would be a religious, patriotic, or other
communal participation encouraged by the style and approach of a quasi-
theatrical production. To the degree that Reinhardt's *The Miracle* (or a
Nuremberg Festival staged by the Nazis or a memorial service for Army and
Navy dead) demanded actual participation rather than disinterested contemplation from the spectator, it was non-aesthetic. This is not meant as a comment on the purpose or effect of any of these, but merely as a description in
terms of art and the theater.

distinguishing between styles and forms of plays. Within these
broad divisions there are of course other categories, historical,
literary, and structural; and each of the latter imposes its own
demands on the director and his actors. The distinctions made
in this section do not settle all the theater artist's problems. But
they do offer pointed suggestions as to how, in general, he
must approach a given play if he is to be at all sure how an
audience is going to *take* it.

Suggestions for Study and Memorization

FOR THE BEGINNING ACTOR

The following generalizations on study and memorization describe psychological and aesthetic processes that are in some measure elusive and unpredictable. We are not identical creatures. Some of us "learn" quickly, others more slowly; some of us are more "visual-minded" or perhaps more "auditory-minded" than others; and a device which proves useful and time-saving to one of us may be less satisfactory to our fellows. If individual student-actors can deliver results without apparent recourse to the principles or procedures summarized below, no one may be the loser on that account, since after all nothing succeeds like success. But unless the beginner is very sure of his ground and can guarantee efficient and dependable methods of his own, he will do well to follow the common experience of his predecessors, as briefly outlined here.[1]

1. *Start on time.* Last-minute preparations are a handicap in many activities; they are doubly so in play production. If you postpone too many of your basic tasks until the last week before performance, you may be forced to work wholly under speed and pressure and may never adequately learn at all. From the beginning, study *before* and *between* rehearsals, not only at them. Remember also that you have an obligation to

[1] Though the present section is of course based principally on my own experience as actor and director, I have had valuable suggestions from students and colleagues in the field, as well as from Frank S. Freeman, Professor of Education and Psychology at Cornell University.

your fellow-actors as well as to your director. One or two ill-prepared actors with delayed reaction-patterns may in the later stages of rehearsal waste everybody else's time — even though they do not quite ruin the production. In general, it is best ultimately to "over-learn"; that is to say, carry your memorization well beyond the point necessary for simple recall. If you can barely repeat your lines as you lie back in an easy-chair, without external distraction, then you must certainly expect to break down from time to time under the varied stimuli of a stage rehearsal.

2. *Know what you are after from the beginning, at least in broad outline; but don't try to do everything at once.* Don't let your patterns of speech and action develop at random, out of odds and ends of other roles or recent unselected off-stage experiences; don't let them just "happen." From personal study and analysis, and from consultation with your director, set up an accurate *first impression* of the sort of thing you are aiming at. If your mind-set in relation to the play, the part, and the director's design is warped from the start — or if you *have* no mind-set — then your learning must inevitably be slow, misdirected, and wasteful. On the whole, try to do what the experienced director tries to do: put first things first. Minor details may fall easily and readily into place during later rehearsals if the broad outlines and the skeletal structure of your job are clarified during the early ones. You cannot hope to be efficient about perfecting detailed business, for example, unless your broad patterns of movement have previously been blocked out and set. If you try to learn everything at once, you may end up by learning nothing at all.

3. *On the other hand, try to relate your learning to a larger context.* Look upon the various aspects of your work as units in a total situation, not as separate items to be considered in isolation. Consider individual lines in the light of the scene in which they appear; study the individual scenes in relation to your part as a whole; and always check your part against the play. Similarly, relate speech to movement, and relate both to your central concept of the character and its dramatic func-

tions. In so far as you are intelligently aware of the broader *meaning* of each line and each movement, they will be easier to learn and harder to forget. Contrariwise, if you "memorize" lines or patterns of movement before you have assimilated their meaning, you may have much to unlearn before the dress rehearsal. In play production, it is best to look upon memorization as considerably more than stereotyped habit-formation; and it is best not to memorize the words, as such, until they can be read in rehearsal with interpretative skill and insight.

4. *As a corollary, try to memorize by wholes, or at least by large units.* Go through the entire scene or act on which you are working several times, focusing closely on the progression of ideas. If you have not already done so, break up the scenes into major units, according to their intellectual or emotional content, and begin the actual memorization by working on these. Do not be deceived by the immediate and tangible results you may achieve by mechanically applying a line-by-line or speech-by-speech method. For most persons, this is the long way around. It promises minor results immediately, but it takes longer in the end; and the consequent reading of the lines is likely to be stereotyped and unexpressive. Naturally enough, you will need to concentrate on details and on specific passages before you are through, but that is quite another matter. The important point here is that you must not be discouraged by an apparent failure to learn easily and rapidly in the early stages of your task, while you are still laying the groundwork for an ultimately effective mastery of the material. Later on you will of course want to set aside several periods for polishing and perfecting details, and for special drill on difficult passages. In the final stages of memorization it is common practice to have a fellow-actor or another student read back essential cues from the manuscript while you are rehearsing, and at the same time check on the perfection of detail which you have thus far achieved in your line-reading.

5. *Whenever possible, study and rehearse the various units of your play essentially as they are sooner or later to be used.* If in practice you breeze through your movements or mumble

over your lines with no thought of expressive content or of integration with fellow-actors and the scene, you are establishing habits that will be of little use to you in stage rehearsals, and you may again be threatening to waste what does not belong to you — other people's time. Should you be forced to use sides, have a copy of the entire manuscript available and refer to it regularly. In particular, do not depend merely on the very last word or two of a preceding line as a cue for speech or action. If you insist on learning only your own lines (and not the *scene*, with all its inter-relationships), you are sure to be at a disadvantage in group rehearsals. Ball players do not learn to bat out home runs by practicing with a window pole; you cannot learn to act unless you practice *acting*, in rehearsals at home as well as on the stage.

6. *Plan your study- and drill-sessions intelligently.* In the first place, space your practice sessions with some care. Long-continued, closely-spaced periods offer diminishing returns for your investment of time and energy, since after a certain point fatigue interferes with efficiency. About two or two and a half hours of continuous, more or less concentrated work are as much as most student-actors can take at one time, particularly if there have been similar periods in the recent past, and particularly if the persons concerned are operating under the pressure of other work. Conversely, brief snatches of less than twenty or thirty minutes of study and drill are likely to prove uneconomical. In short, always work long enough in any one session to get something accomplished, but do not carry the session to the point where you are groggy with fatigue; and, for other but related reasons, do not return to the same task until you have been rested or refreshed, but do not fail to return to it before your partially established habits have been seriously weakened by disuse. If you plan your study and drill adequately, you may be able to cut as much as twenty per cent off your total rehearsal time.

7. *Above all, concentrate.* Study and practice regularly, always with critical alertness and with conscious effort to retain the material you are working on. Active attention is absolutely

essential throughout. Irrelevant distractions or interruptions, divided attention, and uneven concentration on the central task are all wasteful of time and energy. Unless you are rehearsing with a wideawake mind, you might better not be rehearsing at all.

A Glossary and
a Bibliography

FOR THE BEGINNING ACTOR

I. A Glossary of Terms

Above: See *Upstage.*

Act curtain (*Act drop*): The curtain (or drop) used at the beginning and end of entire acts or scenes of a play; in most cases, the permanent house curtain.

Action (*Dramatic action*): The progress of dramatic development, as expressed in dialogue, physical movement, and interrelationship of characters. Distinguish from mere physical action in the narrow sense.

Ad lib (from *ad libitum,* at pleasure): Bits of business and, in particular, lines or speeches not specified in the playscript.

Apron: The portion of the stage on the audience side of the permanent house curtain. Now extremely shallow in typical theaters, it was at one time deep enough to be an important playing area.

Area (*Acting* or *playing area*): One of the several regions into which the onstage space may be arbitrarily divided, as DL, UC, etc.; see pages 115-17. Also: a portion of the onstage space (e.g., before a fireplace DL, around a table C) used for playing an individual scene. Distinguish from *Playing space.*

Aside: A speech, usually brief, which is intended to be heard by the audience but not by the other characters; it may represent a kind of thinking aloud, or may be addressed directly to the audience.

Backdrop: A relatively large sheet of muslin or canvas, used to mask the backstage space in wing settings; attached to a batten at top and bottom, it is hung from the gridiron on a set of lines.

Backing: A flat or series of flats, or a drop, used outside a wall opening (e.g., a window) to mask the backstage space; usually intended to suggest a continuation of the setting, as a hall, another room, a sky, etc.

Backstage: Behind the setting. Or: as distinguished from *Front of the house*, everything behind the proscenium arch.

Balance: See pages 111-12.

Batten: A length of lumber or pipe, usually hung or fastened horizontally across the stage; lights, drops, or other scenery may be attached to battens, or battens may be used to stiffen a back or side wall. (The strips of 1" × 3" lumber used to construct the frame for a standard flat are also called battens.)

Below: See *Downstage*.

Blocking out: Working out basic positions, movements, and relationships in space during early rehearsals.

Border: A relatively short length of canvas or muslin, attached to a batten and hung just above the setting to mask the flies.

Borderlights: A strip or strips of lights (either in an open trough or in individual compartments) hung above the stage to furnish general illumination within the playing space. Compare *Footlights*.

Box set: A standard interior setting of contemporary construction and arrangement, consisting of back and side walls and frequently a ceiling. Distinguish from *wing setting*.

Build: Gradually but insistently to develop a climax of interest or tension, as in a speech or series of speeches, an entire scene, or the play as a whole.

Business: Usually, detailed bits of characteristic action, as in smoking, knitting, setting table, and the like. Distinguish from *stage movement* in the broader sense.

Call: A specific warning to all performers (e.g., "five minutes to curtain") for the beginning of acts or scenes, or to individual actors for an entrance.

Carry: To be clearly seen or heard as well as understood by an audience, as with speeches, movements, business, etc.

Center: As to the center stage area, see pages 115-17. As to centering in line reading, see pages 43-45.

Character parts: Roles dependent on highly specialized and highly individualized characteristics, as opposed to "straight" roles.

Climax: The point of highest interest or tension in speech or pantomime, scene or play.

Color medium: A transparent material (e.g., glass or stage gelatin) placed in front of a spotlight or other source to provide colored light; often in a *color frame*.

Comedy: With *Tragedy,* one of the two basic types of plays; other common types are *Drama, Melodrama,* and *Farce* (which see), usually looked upon as intermediate or extreme forms of the basic ones. A comedy is a play written essentially in a light or humorous vein, with the primary purpose of arousing laughter at the problems or difficulties in which the characters have involved themselves. On the whole a comedy ends happily for most of the persons in the play; and on the whole its dramatic action is dependent on character rather than on merely external incident — this latter distinction setting it off from *Farce.* Note that comedy deals fundamentally with the folly and weakness of men, but that it seeks to arouse laughter, as opposed to concern, or bitterness, or terror. With respect to *theories of comedy,* see the Bibliography.

Cover: To hide from the audience a bit of business, a property, or another actor; may of course be done intentionally under some circumstances.

Cross: To move from place to place on the stage; usually written as "X" (e.g., XDR, XUL).

Cue: The words or pantomime serving as a signal for a reaction that is to follow.

Curtain line: A line across the stage indicating the approximate closed (or dropped) position of the main act curtain. (See also *Exit line.*)

Cyclorama: A curved canvas or muslin background, roughly equivalent to a section of a cylinder, hung from the flies in such a way as to mask most of the sides as well as the back of the offstage space; usually painted or dyed to suggest sky, atmosphere, distance.

Dimmer: A device — usually designed to exploit the principle of electrical resistance, although other types are appearing on the market — for controlling the intensity of light in any given instrument or circuit. (Note that in stage language lights can "dim up" as well as "dim down.")

Downstage: Nearer the audience; downstage areas are also said to be *below* upstage areas.

Drama: A play-type intermediate between *Tragedy* and *Comedy* (which see). A drama is a play of essentially serious intent, without sustained emphasis on the spirit of laughter and play which underlies comedy, but without the inevitability, the elevation, or the impressiveness of tragedy. The broad divisions of serious drama and comedy-drama are sometimes set up, as a further means of characterizing plays which do not achieve or are not intended to achieve full tragic effect on the one hand, or are not wholly comic on the other.

Dress the stage: To keep the stage picture in balance, though not necessarily in formal balance.

Drop: See *Backdrop*.

Exit line: The last words spoken by an actor before he leaves the stage. (On the same principle, note also one sense of *curtain line*.)

Exposition: Explanatory material without which characters, situation, or plot would be unclear; common in, though not necessarily limited to, early scenes.

Extra: A character without lines who may contribute atmosphere or local color, as a passer-by, a member of a crowd, and the like.

Farce: A play which, like a comedy, is expected to arouse laughter, but which stresses external incident and unusual stiuation at the expense of carefully drawn character. Characterizations tend to lack subtlety and plausibility; and effects in general are likely to be exaggerated. The plot is usually fast-moving and more or less arbitrarily contrived.

Feed: To "set up" a laugh-line or climactic effect for another character by unobtrusively supplying or building the preliminary groundwork.

Fire curtain (*Asbestos curtain*): The fireproof curtain (downstage of the permanent act curtain) between stage and house.

Flat: A screen-like unit of flat scenery, consisting of a relatively light wooden frame covered with canvas or muslin; several flats in combination make up the walls of a box set. (A narrow flat is usually called a *jog*.)

Flies: The space above the stage (i.e., beyond the "top" of a setting), in which scenery may be hung or flied on sets of lines.

Floodlight: A lighting instrument, used for general illumination, consisting basically of a large reflector and a high-wattage lamp or several smaller lamps.

Floor cloth: A large sheet of waterproofed duck canvas used as a more or less permanent covering for a stage floor.

Floor plan: A skeleton outline or diagram indicating the position, size, and interrelationship of various parts of the setting, as seen from directly above and with no allowance for perspective.

Fly gallery: A narrow platform or balcony extending along a side wall of a stage at some distance from the floor; the lines used in flying scenery are controlled from the fly gallery.

Footlights: A strip or strips of lights just outside the curtain line, usually in an open trough and usually recessed below the level of the floor, providing general illumination from below. Compare *Borderlights*.

Foreshadow: To indicate or suggest through movement or dialogue a point that may later be of importance in the dramatic action.

Forestage: An elongated apron extending out into the audience space, built for special productions. Or: the downstage portion of the playing space when the stage is divided by an inner proscenium.

Front: In general, the audience and lobby side of the proscenium arch, as in "out front," "front of the house." Distinguish from *Backstage*. Frequently associated with business and house management.

Give: To throw attention to another and more important character or group of characters in a particular scene; may be accomplished, for example, by taking a less conspicuous position on the stage.

Green room: An offstage waiting room for the actors, where they may assemble before or between scenes, wait for a call, and the like.

Grid (Gridiron): A framework of beams, usually steel, near the top of the stage-house; used to support the rigging needed for flying scenery.

Ground cloth: See *Floor cloth*.

Ground plan: See *Floor plan*.

Ground row: A relatively low piece of cut-out scenery whose profile suggests shrubbery, a bank of earth, a distant hill, or the like; usually serves as masking for the bottom of a backdrop or cyclorama.

Hold: To stop all forward movement in speech or action, usually for laughter or applause. (See page 103 on holding for laughs.)

House: In general, the auditorium, lobby, etc., as opposed to stage, workshops, dressing and storage rooms, and green room.

In one: A relatively shallow acting space in a wing setting, including only the space downstage of the first set of wings and their accompanying backdrop. (*In two* includes the space downstage of the second set, and so on.)

Kill: To deprive a line, a bit of business, or a scene of its full and proper effect, as by a distracting or badly-timed movement. Occasionally: to cut out or remove.

Lines: Sets of ropes, usually in groups of three, supported by the gridiron and controlled from the fly gallery, used to hang or fly scenery.

Mask: To conceal from the view of the audience any part of the stage not meant to be seen.

Melodrama: A play stressing suspense and external incident for their own sakes, and usually presenting characters that are typed or at least not fully drawn. The plot is likely to be imposed on the characters for purposes of achieving a more or less striking theatrical effect, and the language and sentiments may lack subtlety as well as normal motivation.

Move on: To move toward center stage from right or left, in roughly the same plane; in the opposite direction one is said to *move off*.

Offstage: Outside the playing space. In any position within the playing space, the actor is said to be *onstage*.

Open: Usually, to turn or to play more directly toward the audience.

Overlap: To speak or move before previous speeches or movements are completed.

Overplay: To give dialogue, movements, or scenes exaggerated emphasis or punch. (*To plug* is often used in a similar way.)

Pace: See *Tempo*.

Pick up: In general, to accelerate. Used frequently as to cues, when the intention is to cut down the interval between the end of one unit and the beginning of another.

Plant: To place and/or call attention to an object or idea that will later be of importance in the action.

Playing space (*Onstage space*): The portion of the stage normally enclosed by the setting, as opposed to *offstage space*. Distinguish from *Acting area*.

Play out: Play more directly toward the audience.

Play up (*Point up*): To focus on, and in various ways stress the importance of, key lines, movements, or scenes.

Plot (*Point*) *lines and business*: See pages 97-98.

Practical: Capable of being used by the actor — as with a tree stump that will bear weight, a window sash that can be raised or lowered, etc.

Prompt side: Traditionally, the side of the stage on which the prompter's or stage manager's desk is located. Note also *O. P.* (i.e., "opposite prompt") *side*.

Properties (*Props*): All furniture and decorative material necessary to the action or required for a complete setting, and all objects used by the actors in the course of a play. Relatively small props handled by the actors are usually called *hand props*, as opposed to *set* or *stage props*. Hand props ordinarily used by a single character are known as *personal props*.

Proscenium: The wall separating the stage and auditorium. Occasionally: the arch in that wall, through which an audience views a production.

Ramp: An inclined platform sloping upward from the stage floor, or connecting any two levels of varying heights.

Return: A flat placed parallel to the footlights and attached to the downstage end of a side wall of a set, running off into the wings behind the tormentor.

Reveal: A thickness piece — as on a door, window, or archway — indicating depth or thickness.

Set: To establish as permanent — through repeated rehearsals — basic patterns of voice or movement.

Share: To assume, in relation to another actor or group of actors, roughly equal dramatic importance in a particular scene. Distinguish from *Give*; *Take*.

Sides: Typed copies of an actor's part, usually just under 6″ × 9″, including only his own speeches, stage directions, and cues.

Soliloquy: A speech, usually of some length, delivered by an actor while he is alone on the stage. Depending on the play and the style of production, the actor may seem to be thinking aloud, or may address the audience more or less directly.

Spotlight: A lighting instrument with a condensing lens, producing specific illumination in a relatively limited area.

Stage brace: A hardwood brace of adjustable length used to support scenery from behind. The top of the brace is hooked into a cleat on the back of a piece of scenery; the bottom of the brace is fastened to the floor by means of a *stage screw* or *peg*.

Stage cable: An electrical conductor made to withstand hard treatment on the stage; its wires, usually two in number, are covered by a heavy outside sheathing as well as by the usual insulation.

Stage left or *right*: The actor's left or right as he faces the house.

Strike: To remove from the onstage space, as a prop or a whole setting.

Striplight: Specifically, a short strip of lights, either in an open trough or in separate compartments, used to light backings and the like. (Sometimes used in reference to any strip of lights, as those in borders or foots.)

Strong or *weak*: Strong or weak in attention-value, as a stage position or movement.

Take: To assume predominant dramatic value in a particular scene, at the expense of other, and for the moment less important, characters. Distinguish from *Give*; *Share*.

Teaser: A neutral-colored border just upstage of the permanent house curtain and just downstage of the tormentors; serves in part to mask the flies, in part to vary the effective height of the proscenium opening.

Telescope: To read lines or perform business simultaneously with other actors.

Tempo: Rate or speed of reading, moving, or playing in general. Usually synonymous with *Pace*.

Throw away: To underplay or underemphasize a line, a bit of business, or a portion of a scene.

Timing: Discovering and setting the precise moment at which lines, business, or movement should be begun, brought into focus, or completed; and planning the precise way in which they should be interrelated.

Top: To emphasize a line or an action (by way of pitch, volume, intensity, or the like), so that it is climactically more effective than a preceding line or action.

Tormentors: Matching, neutral-colored flats or screens placed one on either side of the stage, just upstage of the teaser; they serve in part to mask the wings, in part to vary the effective width of the proscenium opening.

Tragedy: With *Comedy,* one of the two basic types of plays; other common types are *Drama, Melodrama,* and *Farce* (which see), usually looked upon as intermediate or extreme forms of the basic ones. A tragedy is a play written in essentially dark or serious vein, and in elevated or impressive style, with the primary purpose of arousing the profoundest of human emotions, and of leaving the spectator moved but exalted rather than depressed in spirit. On the whole a tragedy ends unhappily for the protagonist, exacting heavy penalties or sacrifices as a result of human weakness or folly. For the most part the dramatic action in a tragedy is dependent on character rather than on merely external incident, a distinction which sets it off from *Melodrama.* With respect to *theories of tragedy,* see the Bibliography.

Trap: A hinged or removable "door" in the floor of a stage.

Upstage: Further from the audience. Upstage areas are also said to be *above* downstage areas.

Wing (Wing-piece): A flat or hinged pair of flats set at the side of a stage, roughly parallel to the footlights, to mask the offstage space. In a backdrop-and-wing setting the wing-pieces are of course painted to represent a public square, a clearing in a forest, a room or hall, and the like.

Wings: Offstage areas to the left and right of the playing space.

II. *A Selected Bibliography*

The following lists are not intended to be exhaustive. Under each heading a group of volumes most useful for the beginner is listed first, with other entries from the same field immediately following. In a few cases an important reference is included under more than one heading. For obvious reasons the entries on acting are more numerous than those in the other categories.

ACTING

Anderson, Virgil A. *Training the Speaking Voice.* New York: Oxford University Press, 1942.

Archer, William. *Masks or Faces?* London: Longmans, Green & Co., 1888.

Boleslavsky, Richard. *Acting: The First Six Lessons.* New York: Theatre Arts, Inc., 1933.

Calvert, Louis. *Problems of the Actor.* New York: Henry Holt & Co., 1918.

Coquelin, Constant. *The Actor and His Art.* Trans. Elsie Fogerty. London: George Allen & Unwin, Ltd., 1932.

Craig, Edward Gordon. *On the Art of the Theatre.* London: William Heinemann, 1911.

D'Angelo, Aristide. *The Actor Creates.* New York: Samuel French, 1939.

Eustis, Morton. *Players at Work.* New York: Theatre Arts, Inc., 1937.

Gillette, William. *The Illusion of the First Time in Acting.* New York: Dramatic Museum of Columbia University, 1915.

Hewitt, Barnard. "The Actor," chapter VIII in *Art and Craft of Play Production.* Philadelphia: J. B. Lippincott Co., 1940.

Kjerbühl-Petersen, Lorenz. *Psychology of Acting.* Trans. Sarah T. Barrows. Boston: The Expression Co., 1935.

Komisarjevsky, Theodore. *Myself and the Theatre.* London: Wm. Heinemann, 1929.

Lewes, George Henry. *On Actors and the Art of Acting.* New York: Brentano's, 1875.

Nichols, Wallace B. *The Speaking of Poetry.* Boston: The Expression Co., 1937.

Parrish, Wayland Maxfield. *Reading Aloud.* Rev. ed. New York: Thomas Nelson & Sons, 1941.

Rosenstein, Sophie, Haydon, Larrae A., and Sparrow, Wilbur. *Modern Acting: A Manual.* New York: Samuel French, 1936.

Selden, Samuel. *A Player's Handbook.* New York: F. S. Crofts & Co., 1934.

Stanislavski, Constantin. *An Actor Prepares.* Trans. Elizabeth Reynolds Hapgood. New York: Theatre Arts, Inc., 1936.

Strasberg, Lee. "Acting and the Training of the Actor," in *Producing the Play.* Ed. John Gassner. New York: The Dryden Press, 1941.

Talma. *Reflexions on the Actor's Art.* New York: Dramatic Museum of Columbia University, 1915.

Young, Stark. *Theatre Practice.* New York: Charles Scribner's Sons, 1926.

Also:

Alberti, Eva Allen. *A Handbook of Acting.* New York: Samuel French, 1932.

Aubert, Charles. *The Art of Pantomime.* Trans. Edith Sears. New York: Henry Holt & Co., 1927.

Bernhardt, Sarah. *The Art of the Theatre.* Trans. H. J. Stenning. London: Geoffrey Bles, Ltd., 1924.

Bosworth, Halliam. *Technique in Dramatic Art.* Rev. ed. New York: The Macmillan Co., 1934.

Boucicault, Dion. *The Art of Acting.* New York: Dramatic Museum of Columbia University, 1926.

Cartmell, Van H. *A Handbook for the Amateur Actor.* Garden City: Doubleday, Doran & Co., 1936.

Colvan, E. B. *Face the Footlights!* New York: McGraw-Hill Book Co., 1940.

Crafton, Allen and Royer, Jessica. *Acting: A Book for Beginners.* New York: F. S. Crofts & Co., 1928.

Franklin, Miriam A. *Rehearsal.* Rev. ed. New York: Prentice-Hall, Inc., 1942.

Herman, Lewis and Herman, Marguerite Shalett. *Manual of Foreign Dialects.* Chicago: Ziff-Davis Publishing Co., 1943.

Lees, C. Lowell. *A Primer of Acting.* New York: Prentice-Hall, Inc., 1940.

Lutz, Florence. *The Technique of Pantomime.* Berkeley: Sather Gate Book Shop, 1927.

Woollcott, Alexander, ed. *Mrs. Fiske, Her Views on Actors, Acting, and the Problems of Production.* New York: The Century Co., 1917.

PLAY PRODUCTION AND DIRECTION

Crafton, Allen and Royer, Jessica. *The Complete Acted Play.* New York: F. S. Crofts & Co., 1943.

Dean, Alexander. *Fundamentals of Play Directing.* New York: Farrar & Rinehart, Inc., 1941.

Dolman, John. *The Art of Play Production.* Rev. ed. New York: Harper & Bros., 1946.

Drummond, A. M. *A Manual of Play Production.* Ithaca, N.Y.: published by the author, 1939.

Heffner, Hubert C., Selden, Samuel, and Sellman, Hunton D. *Modern Theatre Practice.* 3rd ed. New York: F. S. Crofts & Co., 1946.

Hewitt, Barnard. *Art and Craft of Play Production.* Philadelphia: J. B. Lippincott Co., 1940.

Selden, Samuel. *The Stage in Action.* New York: F. S. Crofts & Co., 1941.

Shaw, George Bernard. *The Art of Rehearsal.* New York: Samuel French, 1928.

Also:

Bricker, Herschel, ed. *Our Theatre Today.* New York: Samuel French, 1936.

Brown, Gilmor and Garwood, Alice. *General Principles of Play Direction.* New York: Samuel French, 1937.

Clark, Barrett H. *How to Produce Amateur Plays.* Rev. ed. Boston: Little, Brown & Co., 1925.

Gassner, John, ed. *Producing the Play.* New York: The Dryden Press, 1941.

Smith, Milton. *The Book of Play Production.* New York: D. Appleton & Co., 1926.

AESTHETICS AND DESIGN IN THE THEATER

Bakshy, Alexander. *The Theatre Unbound.* London: Cecil Palmer, 1923.

Centeno, Augusto, ed. *The Intent of the Artist.* Princeton, N.J.: Princeton University Press, 1941.

Dolman, John. *The Art of Play Production.* Rev. ed. New York: Harper & Bros., 1946.

Hewitt, Barnard. *Art and Craft of Play Production.* Philadelphia: J. B. Lippincott Co., 1940.

Langfeld, Herbert Sidney. *The Aesthetic Attitude.* New York: Harcourt, Brace & Co., 1920.

Ogden, Robert Morris. *The Psychology of Art.* New York: Charles Scribner's Sons, 1938.

Prall, D. W. *Aesthetic Judgment.* New York: The Thomas Y. Crowell Co., 1929.

Rader, Melvin M., ed. *A Modern Book of Esthetics.* New York: Henry Holt & Co., 1935.

Selden, Samuel. *The Stage in Action.* New York: F. S. Crofts & Co., 1941.

Also:

Craig, Edward Gordon. *On the Art of the Theatre.* London: William Heinemann, 1911.

————. *Towards a New Theatre.* New York: E. P. Dutton & Co., 1913.

————. *The Theatre Advancing*. Boston: Little, Brown & Co., 1919.

Goldstein, Harriet and Goldstein, Vetta. *Art in Everyday Life*. 3rd ed. New York: The Macmillan Co., 1940.

Moderwell, Hiram Kelly. *The Theatre of To-day*. New York: Dodd, Mead & Co., 1928.

THE DRAMA AND DRAMATIC THEORY

Anderson, Maxwell. *The Essence of Tragedy and Other Footnotes and Papers*. Washington, D.C.: Anderson House, 1939.

Archer, William. *Playmaking*. London: Chapman & Hall, Ltd., 1912.

Baker, George Pierce. *Dramatic Technique*. Boston: Houghton Mifflin Co., 1919.

Bergson, Henri. *Laughter*. Trans. Cloudesley Brereton and Fred Rothwell. New York: The Macmillan Co., 1911.

Bradley, A. C. *Shakespearian Tragedy*. 2nd ed. London: The Macmillan Co., 1937.

Brunetière, Ferdinand. *The Law of the Drama*. New York: Dramatic Museum of Columbia University, 1914.

Clark, Barrett H., ed. *European Theories of the Drama*. Rev. ed. New York: Crown Publishers, 1947.

Cooper, Lane. *Aristotle on the Art of Poetry*. Boston: Ginn & Co., 1913.

Eastman, Max. *Enjoyment of Laughter*. New York: Simon & Schuster, 1936.

Gaw, Allison. "Centers of Interest in Drama, etc.," in *Schelling Anniversary Papers*. New York: The Century Co., 1923.

Lawson, John Howard. *Theory and Technique of Playwriting*. New York: G. P. Putnam's Sons, 1936.

Meredith, George. *An Essay on Comedy and the Uses of the Comic Spirit*. Ed. Lane Cooper. New York: Charles Scribner's Sons, 1918.

Nicoll, Allardyce. *The Theory of Drama*. London: George G. Harrap & Co., Ltd., 1931.

Stuart, Donald Clive. *The Development of Dramatic Art*. New York: D. Appleton & Co., 1928.

Also:

Freud, Sigmund. *Wit and Its Relation to the Unconscious*. Intro. by A. A. Brill. New York: Moffat, Yard & Co., 1916.

Krutch, Joseph Wood. *The Modern Temper*. New York: Harcourt, Brace & Co., 1929.

Maeterlinck, Maurice. "The Tragical in Daily Life," in *The Treasure of the Humble*. Trans. Alfred Sutro. New York: Dodd, Mead & Co., 1903.

Marx, Milton. *The Enjoyment of Drama*. New York: F. S. Crofts & Co., 1940.

Rowe, Kenneth Thorpe. *Write That Play*. New York: Funk & Wagnalls Co., 1939.

THEATER HISTORY AND GENERAL WORKS

Cheney, Sheldon. *The Theatre*. New York: Longmans, Green & Co., 1929.

Freedley, George and Reeves, John A. *A History of the Theatre*. New York: Crown Publishers, 1941.

Gorelik, Mordecai. *New Theatres for Old*. New York: Samuel French, 1941.

Kernodle, George. *From Art to Theatre*. Chicago: University of Chicago Press, 1944.

Nicoll, Allardyce. *The Development of the Theatre*. Rev. ed. New York: Harcourt, Brace & Co., 1937.

Simonson, Lee. *The Stage Is Set*. New York: Harcourt, Brace & Co., 1932.

Stanislavski, Constantin. *My Life In Art*. Trans. J. J. Robbins. Boston: Little, Brown & Co., 1924.

Also:

Hughes, Glenn. *The Story of the Theatre*. New York: Samuel French, 1928.

Komisarjevsky, Theodore. *The Theatre and a Changing Civilization*. London: John Lane, 1935.

Mantzius, Karl. *A History of Theatrical Art*. 6 vols. Trans. Louise von Cossel. London: Duckworth & Co., 1903 ff.

STAGING AND LIGHTING

Barber, Philip. "The New Scene Technician's Handbook," in *Producing the Play*. Ed. John Gassner. New York: The Dryden Press, 1941.

Burris-Meyer, Harold and Cole, Edward C. *Scenery for the Theatre*. Boston: Little, Brown & Co., 1938.

Fuchs, Theodore. *Stage Lighting.* Boston: Little, Brown & Co., 1929.

McCandless, Stanley R. *A Method of Lighting the Stage.* Rev. ed. New York: Theatre Arts, Inc., 1939.

Selden, Samuel and Sellman, Hunton D. *Stage Scenery and Lighting.* Rev. ed. New York: F. S. Crofts & Co., 1936.

Also:

Cornberg, Sol and Gebauer, Emanuel L. *A Stage Crew Handbook.* New York: Harper & Brothers, 1941.

Hake, Herbert V. *Here's How!* Evanston, Ill.: Row, Peterson & Co., 1942.

Helvenston, Harold. *Scenery.* Stanford University: Stanford University Press, 1931.

Nelms, Henning. *Lighting the Amateur Stage.* New York: Theatre Arts, Inc., 1931.

OTHER ASPECTS OF PRODUCTION

Barton, Lucy. *Historic Costume for the Stage.* Boston: Walter H. Baker & Co., 1935.

Corson, Richard. *Stage Make-up.* New York: F. S. Crofts & Co., 1942.

Halstead, William Perdue. *Stage Management for the Amateur Theatre.* New York: F. S. Crofts & Co., 1937.

Napier, Frank. *Noises Off, A Handbook of Sound Effects.* London: Frederick Muller, Ltd., 1936.

Strenkovsky, Serge. *The Art of Make-up.* New York: E. P. Dutton & Co., 1937.

Walkup, Fairfax Proudfit. *Dressing the Part.* New York: F. S. Crofts & Co., 1938.

Whorf, Richard B. and Wheeler, Roger. *Runnin' the Show.* Boston: Walter H. Baker & Co., 1930.

Also:

Baird, John F. *Make-up.* New York: Samuel French, 1930.

Grimball, Elizabeth B. and Wells, Rhea. *Costuming a Play.* New York: The Century Co., 1925.

Komisarjevsky, Theodore. *The Costume of the Theatre.* New York: Henry Holt & Co., 1932.

Smith, Milton. *The Equipment of the School Theatre.* New York: Bureau of Publications, Teachers College, Columbia University, 1930.

INDEXES, BIBLIOGRAPHIES, AND WORKS OF REFERENCE

Baker, Blanch M. *Dramatic Bibliography*. New York: The H. W. Wilson Co., 1933.

Gamble, William Burt. *Development of Scenic Art and Stage Machinery*. New York: New York Public Library, 1928.

Gilder, Rosamond. *A Theatre Library*. New York: Theatre Arts, Inc., 1932.

Ottemiller, John H. *Index to Plays in Collections*. New York: The H. W. Wilson Co., 1943.

Smith, Milton. *Guide to Play Selection*. New York: D. Appleton-Century Co., 1934.

Thonssen, Lester and Fatherson, Elizabeth. *Bibliography of Speech Education*. New York: The H. W. Wilson Co., 1939.

Also:

Bates, Mary E. and Sutherland, Anne C., eds. *Dramatic Index*. Published annually. Boston: F. W. Faxon & Co., 1915 ff.

Firkins, Ina Ten Eyck. *Index to Plays, 1800-1926*. New York: The H. W. Wilson Co., 1927.

————. *Index to Plays, Supplement*. New York: The H. W. Wilson Co., 1935.

Logasa, Hannah and Ver Nooy, Winifred. *An Index to One-Act Plays, 1900-1924*. Boston: F. W. Faxon & Co., 1924.

————. *An Index to One-act Plays. Supplement, 1924-1932*. Boston: F. W. Faxon & Co., 1932.

————. *An Index to One-act Plays. Second Supplement, 1930-1940*. Boston: F. W. Faxon & Co., 1941.

Perry, Clarence Arthur. *The Work of the Little Theatres*. New York: Russell Sage Foundation, 1933.

Sobel, Bernard, ed. *The Theatre Handbook and Digest of Plays*. New York: Crown Publishers, 1943.

Appendix
E

Drill Selections in Reading and Acting

FOR THE BEGINNING ACTOR

I. Poetry and Prose for Reading Aloud

Material of various types, various lengths, and various levels of difficulty is included here. It is expected that much of this material will serve for exercises and drills on voice and articulation, as well as on the projection of intellectual and emotional content, attitude, and the like. In some cases certain of the selections have been specifically assigned in the exercises appearing at the ends of the chapters.

In general, it is best to practice the selections as wholes, and to prepare them for presentation before an actual audience, however small. With occasional exceptions, it is best also to view them as unified projects in communication, rather than as illustrations of special problems in voice quality, articulation, meaning, attitude, and so forth, studied in isolation. In the long run, the several aspects of reading and acting are best learned, most easily criticized, and most readily improved when they are practiced in contextual relation with other aspects of the total problem of communication.

Psalm 23

The Lord is my shepherd; I shall not want.
He maketh me to lie down in green pastures: he leadeth me beside the still waters.
He restoreth my soul: he leadeth me in the paths of righteousness for his name's sake.

Yea, though I walk through the valley of the shadow of death, I will fear no evil: for thou art with me; thy rod and thy staff they comfort me.

Thou preparest a table before me in the presence of mine enemies; thou anointest my head with oil; my cup runneth over.

Surely goodness and mercy shall follow me all the days of my life: and I will dwell in the house of the Lord for ever.

THE PSALMS

Remember Now Thy Creator

Remember now thy Creator in the days of thy youth, while the evil days come not, nor the years draw nigh, when thou shalt say, I have no pleasure in them;

While the sun, or the light, or the moon, or the stars, be not darkened, nor the clouds return after the rain:

In the day when the keepers of the house shall tremble, and the strong men shall bow themselves, and the grinders cease because they are few, and those that look out of the windows be darkened,

And the doors shall be shut in the streets, when the sound of the grinding is low, and he shall rise up at the voice of the bird, and all the daughters of music shall be brought low;

Also when they shall be afraid of that which is high, and fears shall be in the way, and the almond tree shall flourish, and the grasshopper shall be a burden, and desire shall fail; because man goeth to his long home, and the mourners go about the streets:

Or ever the silver cord be loosed, or the golden bowl be broken, or the pitcher be broken at the fountain, or the wheel broken at the cistern.

Then shall the dust return to the earth as it was: and the spirit shall return unto God who gave it.

ECCLESIASTES

From *Life Is a Dream* [1]

We live, while we see the sun,
Where life and dreams are as one;
And living has taught me this
Man dreams the life that is his,
Until his living is done.

[1] Reprinted by permission of Dodd, Mead & Company, Inc.

The king dreams he is king, and he lives
In the deceit of a king,
Commanding and governing;
And all the praise he receives
Is written in wind, and leaves
A little dust on the way
When death ends all with a breath.
Where then is the gain of a throne,
That shall perish and not be known
In the other dream that is death?
Dreams the rich man of riches and fears,
The fears that his riches breed;
The poor man dreams of his need,
And all his sorrows and tears;
Dreams he that prospers with years
Dreams he that feigns and foregoes,
Dreams he that rails on his foes;
And in all the world, I see,
Man dreams whatever he be,
And his own dream no man knows.
And I too dream and behold,
I dream and I am bound with chains,
And I dreamed that these present pains
Were fortunate ways of old.
What is life? a tale that is told;
What is life? a frenzy extreme,
A shadow of things that seem;
And the greatest good is but small,
That all life is a dream to all,
And that dreams themselves are a dream.

CALDERON

(Tr. ARTHUR SYMONS)

Wanderer's Night-Songs [2]

I

Thou that from the heavens art,
Every pain and sorrow stillest,

---

[2] From Longfellow's *Poetical Works*, VI. Reprinted by permission of Houghton Mifflin Company.

And the doubly wretched heart
Doubly with refreshment fillest,
I am weary with contending!
Why this rapture and unrest?
Peace descending
Come, ah, come into my breast!

II

O'er all the hill-tops
Is quiet now,
In all the tree-tops
Hearest thou
Hardly a breath;
The birds are asleep in the trees:
Wait; soon like these
Thou too shalt rest.

GOETHE (Tr. H. W. LONGFELLOW)

From "Aesop's Fables" [3]

The Ass in the Lion's Skin

An Ass put on a Lion's skin and went
About the forest with much merriment,
Scaring the foolish beasts by brooks and rocks,
Till at last he tried to scare the Fox.
But Reynard, hearing from beneath the mane
That raucous voice so petulant and vain,
Remarked, 'O Ass, I too would run away,
But that I know your old familiar bray.'

That's just the way with asses, just the way.

The Swan and the Goose

A rich man bought a Swan and Goose —
That for song, and this for use.
It chanced his simple-minded cook
One night the Swan for Goose mistook.

[3] From *Aesop and Hyssop*, by William Ellery Leonard. Reprinted by permission of Open Court Publishing Co.

But in the dark about to chop
The Swan in two above the crop
He heard the lyric note, and stayed
The action of the fatal blade.

And thus we see a proper tune
Is sometimes very opportune.

(Tr. WILLIAM ELLERY LEONARD)

Composed Upon Westminster Bridge
Sept. 3, 1802

Earth has not anything to show more fair:
Dull would he be of soul who could pass by
A sight so touching in its majesty:
This city now doth like a garment wear
The beauty of the morning; silent, bare,
Ships, towers, domes, theaters, and temples lie
Open unto the fields, and to the sky;
All bright and glittering in the smokeless air.
Never did sun more beautifully steep
In his first splendor, valley, rock, or hill;
Ne'er saw I, never felt, a calm so deep!
The river glideth at his own sweet will:
Dear God! the very houses seem asleep;
And all that mighty heart is lying still!

WILLIAM WORDSWORTH

XXIX

When, in disgrace with fortune and men's eyes,
I all alone beweep my outcast state
And trouble deaf heaven with my bootless cries
And look upon myself and curse my fate,
Wishing me like to one more rich in hope,
Featured like him, like him with friends possessed,
Desiring this man's art and that man's scope,
With what I most enjoy contented least;
Yet in these thoughts myself almost despising,

Haply I think on thee, and then my state,
Like to the lark at break of day arising
From sullen earth, sings hymns at heaven's gate;
For thy sweet love remembered such wealth brings
That then I scorn to change my state with kings.

WILLIAM SHAKESPEARE

From *Childe Harold*

Canto III

I have not loved the world, nor the world me;
I have not flattered its rank breath, nor bowed
To its idolatries a patient knee,
Nor coined my cheek to smiles, nor cried aloud
In worship of an echo; in the crowd
They could not deem me one of such; I stood
Among them, but not of them; in a shroud
Of thoughts which were not their thoughts, and still could,
Had I not filled my mind, which thus itself subdued.

I have not loved the world, nor the world me —
But let us part fair foes; I do believe,
Though I have found them not, that there may be
Words which are things, hopes which will not deceive,
And virtues which are merciful, nor weave
Snares for the failing; I would also deem
O'er others' griefs that some sincerely grieve;
That two, or one, are almost what they seem,
That goodness is no name, and happiness no dream.

LORD BYRON

From *Hyperion*

O tender spouse of gold Hyperion,
Thea, I feel thee ere I see thy face;
Look up, and let me see our doom in it;
Look up, and tell me if this feeble shape
Is Saturn's; tell me, if thou hear'st the voice
Of Saturn; tell me, if this wrinkling brow,

Naked and bare of its great diadem,
Peers like the front of Saturn. Who had power
To make me desolate? whence came the strength?
How was it nurtured to such bursting forth,
While Fate seemed strangled in my nervous grasp?
But it is so; and I am smothered up,
And buried from all godlike exercise
Of influence benign on planets pale,
Of admonitions to the winds, and seas,
Of peaceful sway above man's harvesting,
And all those acts which Deity supreme
Doth ease its heart of love in. — I am gone
Away from my own bosom: I have left
My strong identity, my real self,
Somewhere between the throne, and where I sit
Here on this spot of earth. Search, Thea, search!
Open thine eyes eterne, and sphere them round
Upon all space: space starred, and lorn of light;
Space regioned with life-air; and barren void;
Spaces of fire, and all the yawn of hell. —
Search, Thea, search! and tell me, if thou seest
A certain shape or shadow, making way
With wings or chariot fierce to repossess
A heaven he lost erewhile: it must — it must
Be of ripe progress --Saturn must be King,
Yes, there must be a golden victory;
There must be Gods thrown down, and trumpets blown
Of triumph calm, and hymns of festival
Upon the gold clouds metropolitan,
Voices of soft proclaim, and silver stir
Of strings in hollow shells; and there shall be
Beautiful things made new, for the surprise
Of the sky-children; I will give command:
Thea! Thea! Thea! where is Saturn?

JOHN KEATS

Dover Beach

The sea is calm to-night,
The tide is full, the moon lies fair

Upon the straits; — on the French coast the light
Gleams and is gone; the cliffs of England stand,
Glimmering and vast, out in the tranquil bay,
Come to the window, sweet is the night-air!
Only, from the long line of spray
Where the sea meets the moon-blanched land,
Listen! you hear the grating roar
Of pebbles which the waves draw back, and fling,
At their return, up the high strand,
Begin, and cease, and then again begin,
With tremulous cadence slow, and bring
The eternal note of sadness in.

Sophocles long ago
Heard it on the Aegean, and it brought
Into his mind the turbid ebb and flow
Of human misery; we
Find also in the sound a thought,
Hearing it by this distant northern sea.

The Sea of Faith
Was once, too, at the full, and round earth's shore
Lay like the folds of a bright girdle furled.
But now I only hear
Its melancholy, long, withdrawing roar,
Retreating, to the breath
Of the night-wind, down the vast edges drear
And naked shingles of the world.

Ah, love, let us be true
To one another! for the world, which seems
To lie before us like a land of dreams,
So various, so beautiful, so new,
Hath really neither joy, nor love, nor light,
Nor certitude, nor peace, nor help for pain;
And we are here as on a darkling plain
Swept with confused alarms of struggle and flight,
Where ignorant armies clash by night.

MATTHEW ARNOLD

Vitae Summa Brevis Spem Nos Vetat Incohare Longam [4]

They are not long, the weeping and the laughter,
　　Love and desire and hate:
I think they have no portion in us after
　　We pass the gate.
They are not long, the days of wine and roses:
　　Out of a misty dream
Our path emerges for a while, then closes
　　Within a dream.

ERNEST DOWSON

From The Dark Tower [5]

We shall not always plant while others reap
The golden increment of bursting fruit,
Nor always countenance, abject and mute,
That lesser men should hold their brothers cheap;
Not everlastingly while others sleep
Shall we beguile their limbs with mellow flute,
Not always bend to some more subtle brute.
We were not made eternally to weep.

The night, whose sable breast relieves the stark,
White stars, is no less lovely being dark;
And there are buds that cannot bloom at all
In light, but crumple, piteous, and fall.
So in the dark we hide the heart that bleeds,
And wait, and tend our agonizing seeds.

COUNTEE CULLEN

The End of the World [6]

Quite unexpectedly as Vasserot
The armless ambidextrian was lighting

[4] Reprinted by permission of Dodd, Mead & Company, Inc., and of John Lane, The Bodley Head, Ltd., London.
[5] From *Caroling Dusk,* by Countee Cullen. Copyright, 1927, by Harper & Brothers; reprinted by permission of the publishers.
[6] From *Poems, 1924-1933,* by Archibald MacLeish. Reprinted by permission of Houghton Mifflin Company.

A match between his great and second toe
And Ralph the lion was engaged in biting
The neck of Mme. Sossman while the drum
Pointed, and Teeny was about to cough
In waltz-time swinging Jocko by the thumb —
Quite unexpectedly the top blew off:

And there, there overhead, there, there, hung over
Those thousands of white faces, those dazed eyes,
There in the starless dark, the poise, the hover,
There with vast wings across the cancelled skies,
There in the sudden blackness, the black pall
Of nothing, nothing, nothing — nothing at all.

ARCHIBALD MacLEISH

Pony Rock [7]

One who has loved the hills and died, a man
Intimate with them — how their profiles fade
Large out of evening or through veils of rain
Vanish and reappear or how the sad
Long look of moonlight troubles their blind stones —
One who has loved them does not utterly,
Letting his fingers loosen and the green
Ebb from his eyeballs, close his eyes and go:

But other men long after he is dead
Seeing those hills will catch their breath and stare
As one who reading in a book some word
That calls joy back but can recall not where —
Only the crazy sweetness in the head —
Will stare at the black print till the page is blurred.

ARCHIBALD MacLEISH

Sonnet [8]

Oh! Death will find me, long before I tire
Of watching you; and swing me suddenly

[7] From *Poems, 1924-1933*, by Archibald MacLeish. Reprinted by permission of Houghton Mifflin Company.

[8] From *The Collected Poems of Rupert Brooke*. Copyright, 1915, by Dodd, Mead & Company. Published in Canada by McClelland and Stewart Limited.

Into the shade and loneliness and mire
    Of the last land! There, waiting patiently,

One day, I think, I'll feel a cool wind blowing,
    See a slow light across the Stygian tide,
And hear the Dead about me stir, unknowing,
    And tremble. And I shall know that you have died.

And watch you, a broad-browed and smiling dream,
    Pass, light as ever, through the lightless host,
Quietly ponder, start, and sway, and gleam —
    Most individual and bewildering ghost! —
And turn, and toss your brown delightful head
Amusedly, among the ancient Dead.

RUPERT BROOKE

From *The Pirates of Penzance*

I am the very model of a modern Major-general,
I've information vegetable, animal, and mineral;
I know the kings of England, and I quote the fights historical,
From Marathon to Waterloo, in order categorical;
I'm very well acquainted too with matters mathematical,
About binomial theorem I'm teeming with a lot o' news —
With many cheerful facts about the square of the hypotenuse. . . .
I'm very good at integral and differential calculus,
I know the scientific names of beings animalculous,
In short, in matters vegetable, animal, and mineral,
I am the very model of a modern Major-general.

W. S. GILBERT

From *The Mikado*

To sit in solemn silence in a dull, dark dock,
In a pestilential prison, with a life-long lock,
Awaiting the sensation of a short, sharp shock,
From a cheap and chippy chopper on a big black block!

W. S. GILBERT

From *Patience*

Gentle Jane was as good as gold,
She always did as she was told.
She never spoke when her mouth was full,
Or caught blue-bottles their legs to pull;
Or spilt plum jam on her nice new frock,
Or put white mice in the eight-day clock,
Or vivisected her last new doll,
Or fostered a passion for alcohol.

Teasing Tom was a very bad boy;
A great big squirt was his favorite toy;
He put live shrimps in his father's boots,
And sewed up the sleeves of his Sunday suits;
He punched his poor little sisters' heads,
And cayenne-peppered their four-post beds;
He plastered their hair with cobbler's wax,
And dropped hot halfpennies down their backs.

W. S. GILBERT

From *Ruddigore*

If I were not a little mad and generally silly,
I should give you my advice upon the subject, willy nilly;
I should show you in a moment how to grapple with the question,
And you'd really be astonished at the force of my suggestion.
On the subject I shall write you a most valuable letter,
Full of excellent suggestions when I feel a little better,
But at present I'm afraid I'm as mad as any hatter,
So I'll keep 'em to myself, for my opinion doesn't matter.

W. S. GILBERT

The Gardener's Song [9]

He thought he saw an Elephant
   That practiced on a fife:
He looked again, and found it was
   A letter from his wife.

[9] From *Collected Verse of Lewis Carroll*. Reprinted by permission of E. P. Dutton & Company.

"At length I realize," he said,
"The bitterness of life!"

He thought he saw a Buffalo
　　Upon the chimney-piece:
He looked again, and found it was
　　His Sister's Husband's Niece.
"Unless you leave this house," he said,
　　"I'll send for the Police!"

He thought he saw a Rattlesnake
　　That questioned him in Greek:
He looked again, and found it was
　　The Middle of Next Week.
"The one thing I regret," he said,
　　"Is that it cannot speak!"

He thought he saw a Banker's Clerk
　　Descending from the 'bus:
He looked again, and found it was
　　A Hippopotamus.
"If this should stay to dine," he said,
　　"There won't be much for us!"

He thought he saw a Kangaroo
　　That worked a coffee-mill:
He looked again, and found it was
　　A Vegetable-Pill.
"Were I to swallow this," he said,
　　"I should be very ill!"

He thought he saw a Coach-and-Four
　　That stood beside his bed:
He looked again, and found it was
　　A Bear without a Head.
"Poor thing," he said, "poor silly thing!
　　It's waiting to be fed!"

He thought he saw an Albatross
　　That fluttered round the lamp:

He looked again, and found it was
   A penny-Postage-Stamp.
"You'd best be getting home," he said:
   "The nights are getting damp!"

He thought he saw a Garden Door
   That opened with a key:
He looked again, and found it was
   A Double-Rule-of Three:
"And all its mystery," he said,
   "Is clear as day to me."

LEWIS CARROLL

On *The Romance of History*

The best historians of later times have been seduced from truth, not by their imagination, but by their reason. They far excell their predecessors in the art of deducing general principles from facts. But unhappily they have fallen into the error of distorting facts to suit general principles. They arrive at a theory from looking at some phenomena they strain or curtail to suit the theory. For this purpose it is not necessary that they should assert what is absolutely false; for all questions in morals and politics are questions of comparison and degree. Any proposition which does not involve a contradiction in terms may by possibility be true; and if all the circumstances which raise a probability in its favor be stated and enforced, and those which lead to an opposite conclusion be omitted or lightly passed over, it may appear to be demonstrated. In every human character and transaction there is a mixture of good and evil: a little exaggeration, a little suppression, a judicious use of epithets, a watchful and searching scepticism with respect to the evidence on one side, a convenient credulity with respect to every report or tradition on the other, may easily make a saint of Laud, or a tyrant of Henry IV. . . .

A history in which every particular incident may be true may on the whole be false. The circumstances which have most influence on the happiness of mankind, the changes of manners and morals, the transition of communities from poverty to wealth, from knowledge to ignorance, from ferocity to humanity — these are, for the

most part, noiseless revolutions. Their progress is rarely indicated
by what historians are pleased to call important events. They are
not achieved by armies, or enacted by senates. They are sanc-
tioned by no treaties, and recorded in no archives. They are carried on in every school, in every church, behind ten thousand
counters, at ten thousand firesides. The upper current of society
presents no certain criterion by which we can judge of the direction in which the under current flows. We read of defeats and vic-
tories. But we know that nations may be miserable amidst vic-
tories and prosperous amidst defeats. We read of the fall of wise
ministers and of the rise of profligate favorites. But we must remember how small a proportion the good or evil effected by a
single statesman can bear to the good or evil of a great social
system.

Bishop Watson compares a geologist to a gnat mounted on an
elephant, and laying down theories as to the whole internal structure of the vast animal, from the phenomena of the hide. The comparison is unjust to the geologists; but is very applicable to those
historians who write as if the body politic were homogeneous, who
look only on the surface of affairs, and never think of the mighty
and various organization which lies deep below.

Thomas Babington Macaulay

From *On Familiar Style*

Such persons are in fact besotted with words, and their brains
are turned with the glittering, but empty and sterile phantoms of
things. Personifications, capital letters, seas of sunbeams, visions
of glory, shining inscriptions, the figures of a transparency, Bri-
tannia with her shield, or Hope leaning on an anchor, make up
their stock in trade. They may be considered as *hieroglyphical*
writers. Images stand out in their minds isolated and important
merely in themselves, without any ground-work of feeling — there
is no context in their imaginations. Words affect them in the same
way, by the mere sound, that is, by their possible, not by their
actual application to the subject in hand. They are fascinated by
first appearances, and have no sense of consequences. Nothing
more is meant by them than meets the ear: they understand or feel
nothing more than meets their eye. The web and texture of the

universe, and of the heart of man, is a mystery to them: they have no faculty that strikes a chord in unison with it. They cannot get beyond the daubings of fancy, the varnish of sentiment. Objects are not linked to feelings, words to things, but images revolve in splendid mockery, words represent themselves in their strange rhapsodies. The categories of such a mind are pride and ignorance — pride in outside show, to which they sacrifice everything, and ignorance of the true worth and hidden structure both of words and things. With a sovereign contempt for what is familiar and natural, they are the slaves of vulgar affectation — of a routine of high-flown phrases. Scorning to imitate realities, they are unable to invent anything, to strike out one original idea. They are not copyists of nature, it is true: but they are the poorest of all plagiarists, the plagiarists of words. All is far-fetched, dear-bought, artificial, oriental in subject and allusion: all is mechanical, conventional, vapid, formal, pedantic in style and execution. They startle and confound the understanding of the reader, by the remoteness and obscurity of their illustrations: they soothe the ear by the monotony of the same everlasting round of circuitous metaphors. They are the *mock-school* in poetry and prose. They flounder about between fustian in expression, and bathos in sentiment. They tantalize the fancy, but never reach the head nor touch the heart. Their Temple of Fame is like a shadowy structure raised by Dullness to Vanity, or like Cowper's description of the Empress of Russia's palace of ice, "as worthless as in show 'twas glittering" —

It smiled, and it was cold!

WILLIAM HAZLITT

From *The Double Barreled Detective Story* [10]

It was a crisp and spicy morning in early October. The lilacs and laburnums, lit with the glory fires of autumn, hung burning and flashing in the upper air, a fairy bridge provided by kind nature for the wingless wild things that have their home in the tree-tops and would visit together; the larch and the pomegranate flung their purple and yellow flames in brilliant broad splashes along the slanting sweep of woodland, the sensuous fragrance of

[10] Reprinted by permission of Harper and Brothers.

innumerable deciduous flowers rose upon the swooning atmosphere, far in the empty sky a solitary oesophagus slept upon motionless wing; everywhere brooded stillness, serenity, and the peace of God.

MARK TWAIN

From *Note Books* [11]

O Critics, cultured critics!
Who will praise me after I am dead,
Who will see in me both more and less than I intended,
But who will swear that whatever it was it was all perfectly right:
You will think you are better than the people who, when I was
      alive, swore that whatever I did was wrong,
And damned my books for me as fast as I could write them;
But you will not be better, you will be just the same, neither better,
      nor worse,
And you will go for some future Butler as your fathers have gone
      for me:
O, how I should have hated you!
But you, nice People!
Who will be sick of me because the critics thrust me down your
      throats,
But who would take me willingly enough if you were not bored
      about me,
Or if you could have the cream of me — and surely this should
      suffice:
Please remember that if I were living, I should have been upon
      your side,
And should hate those who imposed me either on myself or others;
Therefore, I pray you, neglect me, burlesque me, boil me down, do
      whatever you like with me,
But do not think that, if I were living, I should not Aid and abet
      you:
There is nothing that even Shakespeare would enjoy more than a
      good burlesque of Hamlet.

SAMUEL BUTLER

[11] From Butler's *Works*, Shrewsbury edition. Reprinted by permission of E. P. Dutton & Co.

From *A Bottomless Grave* [12]

My father, a drunkard, had a patent for an invention for making coffee-berries out of clay; but he was an honest man and would not himself engage in the manufacture. He was, therefore, only moderately wealthy, his royalties from his really valuable invention bringing him hardly enough to pay his expenses of litigation with rogues guilty of infringement. So I lacked many advantages enjoyed by the children of unscrupulous and dishonorable parents, and had it not been for a noble and devoted mother, who neglected all my brothers and sisters and personally supervised my education, should have grown up in ignorance and been compelled to teach school. To be the favorite child of a good woman is better than gold.

When I was nineteen years of age my father had the misfortune to die. He had always had perfect health, and his death, which occurred at the dinner table without a moment's warning, surprised no one more than himself. He had that very morning been notified that a patent had been granted him for a device to burst open safes by hydraulic pressure, without noise. The Commissioner of Patents had pronounced it the most ingenious, effective and generally meritorious invention that had ever been submitted to him, and my father had naturally looked forward to an old age of prosperity and honor. His sudden death was, therefore, a deep disappointment to him; but my mother, whose piety and resignation to the will of Heaven were conspicuous virtues of her character, was apparently less affected.

AMBROSE BIERCE

From *All Arted Uppe* [13]

I took the long count of seventeen one day in Illinois when I ran across a sign attached to a tea room and gift shop which read:

YE OLDE GRISTE MILLE

The building sat beside the road under some fine elm trees, in a fertile prairie country. I halted Ye Antique Motor Carre, and be-

[12] From *Negligible Tales,* in *The Collected Writings of Ambrose Bierce.* Reprinted by permission of The Citadel Press, New York.
[13] From *The American Magazine,* January, 1929. Reprinted by permission.

gan to investigate for some sign of a brook, creek, run, branch, or river in the neighborhood. There wasn't any, and there never had been any. I was born and brought up in Illinois myself, and I didn't remember having seen any water mills sitting out on the Illinois prairies when I was a kid. Ye typical Olde Village Mille in Illinois would have been a steam mill. . . .

Not far from this mill, located where no stream had ever been, I came upon:

YE OLDE BLUE COWE

And for a moment I was startled. My father used to own the only blue cow I ever knew, and in that same part of Illinois. She was of the Holstein family, and her blueness was amazing. I wondered, for a flurried instant, if she could be still alive and had taken to running a tea room in her old age. But I soon saw that the proprietress was a calfless spinster. . . .

Now and then, along with ye windmills, the weird dishes, the art jewelry made of sealing wax, the fake ship models, the tin cans, one runs upon a sign which shows a faint indication in the proprietor to kid the game himself — or, more usually, herself. Here is one from a New Jersey shop:

YE OLDE HOOPE SKIRTE

And the wire skeleton of one of those strange old garments, gilded, was hanging in front of ye shoppe. The Yellow Sunflower is near Schenectady, New York, although it ought to be in Kansas, I should think. Another bit of facetious honesty comes from Long Island:

YE OLDE JUNKE SHOPPE

And one honest citizen of Connecticut advertises that he is prepared to make duplicates and imitations of old furniture, in any pattern, out of new, sound wood.

If I see a wooden-legged man sitting in front of a country crossroads store these days, I drive hurriedly by before he has a chance to roll up his trouser to the knee and display it as an *objet d'art* or an authentic antique to me. For I am certain that it will have portraits of his ancestors, or a picture of a ship, or perhaps his age and pedigree, painted upon it; or else, in sprawling red letters:

YE OLDE PEGGE LEGGE

Maybe I'm just an old crab, but, personally, I've never seen much of this arted uppe stuff I wanted to take home with me. It hurts my digestion. I'd rather look at tire and cigarette ads.

Don Marquis

From *The Moralist in an Unbelieving World* [14]

In an age when custom is dissolved and authority is broken, the religion of the spirit is not merely a possible way of life. In principle it is the only way which transcends the difficulties. It alone is perfectly neutral about the constitution of the universe, in that it has no expectation that the universe will justify naïve desire. Therefore, the progress of science cannot upset it. Its indifference to what the facts may be is indeed the very spirit of scientific inquiry. A religion which rests upon particular conclusions in astronomy, biology, and history may be fatally injured by the discovery of new truths. But the religion of the spirit does not depend upon creeds and cosmologies; it has no vested interest in any particular truth. It is concerned not with the organization of matter, but with the quality of human desire. . . .

The philosophy of the spirit is an almost exact reversal of the worldling's philosophy. The ordinary man believes that he will be blessed if he is virtuous, and therefore virtue seems to him a price he pays now for a blessedness he will some day enjoy. While he is waiting for his reward, therefore, virtue seems to him drab, arbitrary, and meaningless. . . . (But) in the realm of the spirit, blessedness is not deferred: there is no future which is more auspicious than the present; there are no compensations later for evils now. Evil is to be overcome now and happiness is to be achieved now, for the kingdom of God is within you. The life of the spirit is not a commercial transaction in which the profit has to be anticipated; it is a kind of experience which is inherently profitable.

And so the mature man would take the world as it comes, and within himself remain quite unperturbed. When he acted, he would know that he was only testing an hypothesis, and if he failed, he would know that he had made a mistake. He would be quite pre-

[14] From *A Preface to Morals*, by Walter Lippmann. By permission of The Macmillan Company, publishers.

pared for the discovery that he might make mistakes, for his intelligence would be disentangled from his hopes. The failure of his experiment could not, therefore, involve the failure of his life. . . . Since nothing gnawed at his vitals, neither doubt nor ambition, nor frustration, nor fear, he would move easily through life. And so whether he saw the thing as comedy, or high tragedy, or plain farce, he would affirm that it is what it is, and that the wise man can enjoy it.

....   WALTER LIPPMANN

From *Through Space and Time* [15]

Imagine that we stand on any ordinary seaside pier, and watch the waves rolling in and striking against the iron columns of the pier. Large waves pay very little attention to the columns — they divide right and left and re-unite after passing each column, much as a regiment of soldiers would if a tree stood in their road; it is almost as though the columns had not been there. But the short waves and ripples find the columns of the pier a much more formidable obstacle. When the short waves impinge on the columns, they are reflected back and spread as new ripples in all directions. To use the technical term, they are "scattered." The obstacle provided by the iron columns hardly affects the long waves at all, but scatters the short ripples.

We have been watching a sort of working model of the way in which sunlight struggles through the earth's atmosphere. Between us on earth and outer space the atmosphere interposes innumerable obstacles in the form of molecules of air, tiny droplets of water, and small particles of dust. These are represented by the columns of the pier.

The waves of the sea represent the sunlight. We know that sunlight is a blend of lights of many colours — as we can prove for ourselves by passing it through a prism, or even through a jug of water, or as Nature demonstrates to us when she passes it through the raindrops of a summer shower and produces a rainbow. We also know that light consists of waves, and that the different colours of light are produced by waves of different lengths, red light by

[15] From *The Stars in Their Courses*, by Sir James Jeans. By permission of The Macmillan Company, publishers, and The University Press, Cambridge.

long waves and blue light by short waves. The mixture of waves which constitutes sunlight has to struggle through the obstacles it meets in the atmosphere, just as the mixture of waves at the seaside has to struggle past the columns of the pier. And these obstacles treat the light-waves much as the columns of the pier treat the sea-waves. The long waves which constitute red light are hardly affected, but the short waves which constitute blue light are scattered in all directions.

Thus, the different constituents of sunlight are treated in different ways as they struggle through the earth's atmosphere. A wave of blue light may be scattered by a dust particle, and turned out of its course. After a time a second dust particle again turns it out of its course, and so on, until finally it enters our eyes by a path as zigzag as that of a flash of lightning. Consequently the blue waves of the sunlight enter our eyes from all directions. And that is why the sky looks blue.

SIR JAMES JEANS

From *A Look Around* [16]

Let us glance at some of the . . . queer creatures created by personifying abstractions in America. Here in the center is a vast figure called the Nation — majestic and wrapped in the Flag. When it sternly raises its arm, we are ready to die for it. Close behind rears a sinister shape, the Government. Following it is one even more sinister, Bureaucracy. Both are festooned with the writhing serpents of Red Tape. High in the heavens is the Constitution, a kind of chalice like the Holy Grail, suffused with ethereal light. It must never be joggled. Below floats the Supreme Court, a black-robed priesthood tending the eternal fire. The Supreme Court must be addressed with respect or it will neglect the fire and the Constitution will go out. This is synonymous with the end of the world. Somewhere above the Rocky Mountains are lodged the vast stone tablets of the Law. We are governed not by men but by these tablets. Near them, in satin breeches and silver buckles, pose the stern figures of our Forefathers, contemplating glumly the Nation they brought to birth. The onion-shaped demon cowering behind the

[16] From *The Tyranny of Words*, by Stuart Chase. Reprinted by permission of Harcourt, Brace and Company, publishers.

Constitution is Private Property. Higher than Court, Flag, or the Law, close to the sun itself and almost as bright, is Progress, the ultimate God of America. . . .

Here are the Masses, thick, black, and squirming. This demon must be firmly sat upon; if it gets up, terrible things will happen; the Constitution may be joggled — anything. Capital, her skirts above her knees, is preparing to leave the country at the drop of a hairpin, but never departs. Skulking from city to city goes Crime, a red, loathsome beast, upon which the Law is forever trying to drop a monolith, but its aim is poor. Crime continues rhythmically to Rear Its Ugly Head. Here is the dual shape of Labor — for some a vast, dirty, clutching hand, for others a Galahad in armor. Pacing to and fro with remorseless tread are the Trusts and the Utilities, bloated, unclean monsters with enormous biceps. Here is Wall Street, a crouching dragon ready to spring upon assets not already nailed down in any other section of the country. The Consumer, a pathetic figure in a gray shawl, goes wearily to market. Capital and Labor each give her a kick as she passes, while Commercial Advertising, a playful sprite, squirts perfume into her eyes. . . .

Such, gentlemen, is the sort of world which our use of language fashions.

STUART CHASE

From *Credo* [17]

I believe that we are lost here in America, but I believe we shall be found. . . .

I think the true discovery of America is before us. I think the true fulfillment of our spirit, of our people, of our mighty and immortal land, is yet to come. I think the true discovery of our own democracy is still before us. And I think that all these things are certain as the morning, as inevitable as noon. I think I speak for most men living when I say that our America is Here, is Now, and beckons on before us, and that this glorious assurance is not only our living hope, but our dream to be accomplished.

I think the enemy is here before us, too. But I think we know the forms and faces of the enemy, and in the knowledge that we

[17] From *You Can't Go Home Again,* by Thomas Wolfe. Reprinted by permission of Harper & Brothers.

know him, and shall meet him, and eventually must conquer him is also our living hope. I think the enemy is here before us with a thousand faces, but I think we know that all his faces wear one mask. I think the enemy is single selfishness and compulsive greed. . . .

I think the enemy comes to us with the face of innocence and says to us:

"I am your friend. . . ."

He lies! And now we know he lies! He is not gloriously, or in any other way, ourselves. He is not our friend, our son, our brother. And he is not American! For, although he has a thousand familiar and convenient faces, his own true face is old as Hell.

Look about you and see what he has done.

Dear Fox, old friend, thus we have come to the end of the road that we were to go together. My tale is finished — and so farewell.

But before I go, I have just one more thing to tell you:

Something has spoken to me in the night, burning the tapers of the waning year; something has spoken in the night, and told me I shall die, I know not where. Saying:

"To lose the earth you know, for greater knowing; to lose the life you have, for greater life; to leave the friends you loved, for greater loving; to find a land more kind than home, more large than earth —

" — Whereon the pillars of this earth are founded, toward which the conscience of the world is tending — a wind is rising, and the rivers flow."

THOMAS WOLFE

From *Look Homeward, Angel!* [18]

. . . a stone, a leaf, an unfound door; of a stone, a leaf, a door. And of all the forgotten faces.

Naked and alone we came into exile. In her dark womb we did not know our mother's face; from the prison of her flesh have we come into the unspeakable and incommunicable prison of this earth.

Which of us has known his brother? Which of us has looked into his father's heart? Which of us has not remained forever prison-pent? Which of us is not forever a stranger and alone?

O waste of loss, in the hot mazes, lost, among bright stars on this most weary unbright cinder, lost! Remembering speechlessly we seek the great forgotten language, the lost lane-end into heaven, a stone, a leaf, an unfound door. Where? When?

O lost, and by the wind grieved, ghost, come back again.

THOMAS WOLFE

From *Confessions of a Gallomaniac* [19]

Then began a career of hypocritical benevolence. I scraped acquaintance with every Frenchman whom I heard talking English very badly, and I became immensely interested in his welfare. I formed the habit of introducing visiting Frenchmen to French-speaking Americans, and sitting, with open mouth, in the flow of their conversation. Then I fell in with M. Bernou, the commissioner who was over here buying guns, and whose English and my French were so much alike that we agreed to interchange them. We met daily for two weeks and walked for an hour in the park, each tearing at the other's language. Our conversations, as I look back on them, must have run about like this:

"It calls to walk," said he, smiling brilliantly.

"It is good morning," said I, "better than I had extended."

"I was at you yestairday ze morning, but I deed not find."

"I was obliged to leap early," said I, "and I was busy standing up straight all around the forenoon."

"The book I prayed you send, he came, and I thank, but positively are you not deranged?"

"Don't talk," said I. "Never talk again. It was really nothing anywhere. I had been very happy, I reassure."

"Pardon, I glide, I glode. There was the hide of a banane. Did I crash you?"

"I noticed no insults," I replied. "You merely gnawed my arm."

Gestures and smiles of perfect understanding.

I do not know whether Bernou, who like myself was middle-aged, felt as I did on these occasions, but by the suppression of every thought that I could not express in my childish vocabulary, I came to feel exactly like a child. They said I ought to think in French

[19] Reprinted by permission of Dodd, Mead & Company, Inc.

and I tried to do so, but thinking in French, when there is so little French to think with, divests the mind of its acquisitions of forty years. Experience slips away for there are not words enough to lay hold of it. Knowledge of good and evil does not exist; the sins have no names; and the mind under its limitations is like a rather defective toy Noah's ark. From the point of view of Bernou's and my vocabulary, Central Park was as the Garden of Eden after six months — new and unnamed things everywhere. A dog, a tree, a statue taxed all our powers of description, and on a complex matter like a policeman our minds could not meet at all. We could only totter together a few steps in any mental direction. Yet there was a real pleasure in this earnest interchange of insipidities and they were highly valued on each side. For my part I shall always like Bernou, and feel toward him as my childhood's friend. I wonder if he noticed that I was an old, battered man, bothered with a tiresome profession. I certainly never suspected that he was. His language utterly failed to give me that impression.

FRANK MOORE COLBY

II. Scenes for Rehearsal and Informal Presentation

The ten scenes included here range in mood from what could be broadly described as light to serious. They are relatively uniform in length and, generally speaking, in difficulty. Each scene is well balanced as to the "importance" of the roles, and is therefore to that degree balanced in regard to its potential value as an exercise for individual actors. Each is just long enough to present a real task of assimilation and projection, though not so long as to require a disproportionate amount of time for preparation. Each in its own way offers a dramatic situation that can test — in action — the beginner's knowledge, skill, and insight.

It is in the nature of things that these scenes are exercises or drills and not plays in process of production, and that therefore they have certain recognizable limitations. On the other hand, if they are properly used, they afford the student valuable training and experience under controlled conditions suitable to a beginner's problems and a beginner's approach.

Except for experimental purposes (e.g., Exercise X of Chapter 6) none of the scenes should be presented by actors unfamiliar with the context from which it has been extracted. The preliminary material, printed in brackets, which precedes each scene is in no sense orientation for proper study and rehearsal. This material may serve, however, as a point of departure in preparing introductory remarks for the audience at the time of presentation. It is expected that the scenes will normally be given informally and without more or less elaborate production aids, although in some cases characteristic props, costumes, and make-up may well be suggested. Emphasis throughout should be on the acting, where it rightfully belongs under the circumstances; and judgments of success should be based on qualities inherent in the speech, the movement, and the interpretation.

These scenes are of course included here only for purposes of class analysis and drill; in their present form they are not intended for public performance, and cannot be so presented without the usual special permission from the agents concerned.

FIRST LADY [20]

For 1 man; 1 woman

KATHARINE DAYTON and GEORGE S. KAUFMAN

[CARTER HIBBARD'S *study. Walls lined with bookcases filled with books that are obviously "in re" or "vs." something. Law reports, reference works, etc. Classical busts on top of bookcases, and, by way of contrast, a great mounted fish — a particularly homely fish, so realistically stuffed that you can almost hear it gasp.*

In the biggest of the chairs, left, sits CARTER HIBBARD, *Associate Justice of the Supreme Court. In his sixties — dignified, solemn. A pile of law journals and Congressional Records at his elbow. He looks at his watch; makes a little rumbling sound and pats his stomach. Adjusts his glasses. Takes a soda tablet.*

[20] Copyright, 1935, by George S. Kaufman and Katharine Dayton. Reprinted by permission of Random House, Inc.

At the other side of the room IRENE HIBBARD *sits regarding him. Resplendent in evening clothes, obviously not donned just to sit home with Carter Hibbard. Jeweled sandals reveal toes.*

The radio has been playing, and CARTER *has been fooling with the dials.*]

IRENE.   Carter.

HIBBARD.   H'm?

IRENE.   (*Shouting above din of the radio*) I'm going to Middleburg over the week-end. The Anthonys.

HIBBARD... What?

IRENE.   (*Still shouting, although* CARTER *has toned down the radio*) I'm going to spend the week-end with the Anthonys. In Middleburg.

HIBBARD.   (*He looks up.*) *This* week-end? Saturday is the Chief Justice's dinner.

IRENE.   Well, what *of* it?

HIBBARD.   What of it? We must go there together. There are two places that we must always go together — the Chief Justice's and the White House.

IRENE.   The Chief Justice's dinners bore me to death. Habeas corpus, and you're home again at ten-thirty. And the Anthonys are having a very amusing crowd.

HIBBARD.   That's beside the point. The Chief Justice is the Chief Justice. (*Looks at his newspaper.*) (*Suddenly he is reminded of an amusing incident in the day's work.*) He was very perturbed today. You should have been there. Henshaw contended that a judgment resting on service by publication was not valid as a judgment in persona. A most interesting case. I brought the briefs home with me. (*At desk*) Now, where are those papers? (*He is looking around, seeking papers on his desk.*)

IRENE.   I ate them. (*Quite calmly*)

HIBBARD.   How's that?

IRENE.   I ate them.

HIBBARD.   My dear, you're behaving very peculiarly to-night. . . . [*He goes back to the dials.*]

IRENE.   (*As the Whoops Family theme song is softly played over the radio, rises.*) Carter, will you turn that off, please? (*Crosses to R.*)

HIBBARD.   (*As he dials down*) Turn it off? Irene, you know very well that after the grind of the day's work the clean wholesome fun of the Whoops Family —

IRENE. Relaxes you! I know! And when you're relaxed you stay relaxed until Bleecker brings your Ovaltine, and that relaxes you *again!* And then you go to bed, and GOD! how you relax!

HIBBARD. That is an unreasonable contention, my dear. The greatest minds in history required relaxation. Take Abraham Lincoln. He too relished an occasional bit of humor.

IRENE. Yes, Carter. But you have all of Lincoln's annoying qualities and none of his great ones.

HIBBARD. (*Aghast*) Really, my dear! [*He listens, as a radio voice continues:*] Good evening, folks! What is it that gives that lovely, sweet taste to the mouth when little tousle-heads make ready for another day? It is Dr. Mackintosh's Sweet-Wheaties, especially prepared for the ——

(*Irene, in a fury, strides to the radio and snaps it off.*)

HIBBARD. (*Rises.*) (*On his feet*) Irene!

IRENE. I'm through, Carter.

HIBBARD. What's that?

IRENE. I'm through. Through, done, finished!

HIBBARD. My dear, this is a most unseemly exhibition.

IRENE. Oh, come down off that bench! Stop being a Supreme Court judge and be a human being just long enough to *understand* this. I'm leaving you, Carter. I'm leaving you because I can't stand it — one — minute — longer.

HIBBARD. You don't know what you're saying! Because I turned on the radio?

IRENE. (*In an unnatural voice*) Yes! Because you turned on the radio. That's as good a reason as any.

HIBBARD. But that's absurd. That wouldn't stand in a court of law.

IRENE. (*Pacing*) Law, law! What's law got to do with marriage? What's law compared to the Whoops Family, and those briefs you bring home, and that fish up on the wall, and that kit of tools that you carry in your pocket, and your stomach, stomach, stomach! What's law got to do with your stomach! Answer me that!

HIBBARD. So! This is a case of incompatibility!

IRENE. And sitting here night after night! Night after night after night after night after night! Relaxing!

HIBBARD. (*Finally stung*) You haven't sat here very many nights.

Traipsing around with young Keane all over the place! How about *that?*

IRENE. Well, Senator Keane — !

HIBBARD. Is it my stomach or Senator Keane that's at the root of this? I suppose he hasn't *got* a stomach!

IRENE. I never should have married a man so much older.

HIBBARD. (*Crossing to her*) You're not so young any more. You haven't been able to look up a telephone number for five years!

IRENE. Leave my age out of this!

HIBBARD. You tried marrying a younger man. That didn't work so well either.

IRENE. Leave my marriage out of it, too!

HIBBARD. You bought your rotten little Prince Gregoravitch and then you had to buy the filthy Slovanian courts to get rid of him — when I think of myself mixing in that mess! You were just as eager then for respectability and security as you are now to escape from them! Well, I've given them to you! The daughter of Sockless Sam Baker is the wife of a Supreme Court Justice!

IRENE. You leave my father out of this!

HIBBARD. Sockless Sam Baker! Never took a spoon out of a coffee cup! And I've given you a social position second to none! (*He crosses back to the desk.*)

IRENE. Thank you so much. It's so courteous of you to remind me. And I suppose I didn't *buy you,* too, as you so delicately put it? All those years when you were counsel for Baker Steamers. Doing *their* dirty work!

HIBBARD. Irene, you know my stomach. You know what those scenes do to me, a man with my constitution. (*Sinks in the desk chair.*)

IRENE. (*Crossing to him*) Constitution! If it isn't *your* constitution it's the country's — I don't know which is the more deadly! All I know is that I'm sick of them both! I'm sick of *you,* if you must know! And you don't want me! You've got your Supreme Court and your fish — that's all you care about! Just be careful that you don't get them mixed up! (*Crosses to R.*)

HIBBARD. (*Rises.*) That will do, Irene. You have chosen to cast aspersion upon my calling — the highest and noblest in all the world. It is an offense I can neither forgive nor condone.

IRENE. (*Crosses to C.*) That suits me, as long as you understand the situation. I want a divorce and I want it quickly. You got me one when you were a dinkey Cleveland lawyer; it ought to be easy for a Supreme Court Judge.

HIBBARD. You'll get your divorce — Go! And take that fancy chef with you. No one will reproach *me*; before the bar of public opinion, the onus will be borne by you. (*A step to her*)

IRENE. Onus! Onus! Do you think anyone cares what the wife of a Supreme Court Judge does? Do you think anyone even knows that a Supreme Court Judge has a wife? Do you suppose a Supreme Court Justice is credited with any passion stronger than *heartburn!*

HIBBARD. (*With enormous dignity*) The discussion is at an end.

[*Act II, Scene i*]

THE LITTLE FOXES 21

For 1 man; 1 woman

LILLIAN HELLMAN

[*The living room of the Giddens house. It is late afternoon and it is raining.* HORACE *is sitting near the window in a wheel chair. On the table near him is a safe deposit box, and a bottle of medicine.*

REGINA *has just come into the hall, shaken out her umbrella, thrown her cloak over the banister, etc. As she enters the room, she stares at* HORACE.]

REGINA. (*As she takes off her gloves*) We had agreed that you were to stay in your part of this house and I in mine. This room is *my* part of the house. Please don't come down here again.

HORACE. I won't.

REGINA. (*Crosses towards bell-cord.*) I'll get Cal to take you upstairs.

HORACE. (*Smiles.*) Before you do I want to tell you that after all, we have invested our money in Hubbard Sons and Marshall, Cotton Manufacturers.

REGINA. (*Stops, turns, stares at him.*) What are you talking about? You haven't seen Ben — When did you change your mind?

HORACE. I didn't change my mind. *I* didn't invest the money. (*Smiles.*) It was invested for me.

REGINA. (*Angrily*) What — ?

HORACE. I had eighty-eight thousand dollars' worth of Union Pacific bonds in that safe-deposit box. They are not there now. Go and look. (*As she stares at him, he points to the box.*) Go and look, Regina. (*She crosses quickly to the box, opens it.*) Those bonds are as negotiable as money.

REGINA. (*Turns back to him.*) What kind of joke are you playing now? Is this for my benefit?

HORACE. I don't look in that box very often, but three days ago, on Wednesday it was, because I had made a decision —

REGINA. I want to know what you are talking about.

HORACE. (*Sharply*) Don't interrupt me again. Because I had made a decision, I sent for the box. The bonds were gone. Eighty-eight thousand dollars gone. (*He smiles at her.*)

REGINA. (*After a moment's silence, quietly*) Do you think I'm crazy enough to believe what you're saying?

HORACE. (*Shrugs.*) Believe anything you like.

REGINA. (*Stares at him, slowly.*) Where did they go to?

HORACE. They are in Chicago. With Mr. Marshall, I should guess.

REGINA. What did they do? Walk to Chicago? Have you really gone crazy?

HORACE. Leo took the bonds.

REGINA. (*Turns sharply, then speaks softly, without conviction.*) I don't believe it.

HORACE. (*Leans forward.*) I wasn't there but I can guess what happened. This fine gentleman, to whom you were willing to marry your daughter, took the keys and opened the box. You remember that the day of the fight Oscar went to Chicago? Well, he went with my bonds that his son Leo had stolen for him. (*Pleasantly*) And for Ben, of course, too.

REGINA. (*Slowly, nods.*) When did you find out the bonds were gone?

HORACE. Wednesday night.

REGINA. I thought that's what you said. Why have you waited three days to do anything? (*Suddenly laughs.*) This *will* make a fine story.

HORACE. (*Nods.*) Couldn't it?

REGINA. (*Still laughing*) A fine story to hold over their heads. How could they be such fools? (*Turns to him.*)

HORACE. But I'm not going to hold it over their heads.

REGINA. (*The laugh stops.*) What?

HORACE. (*Turns his chair to face her.*) I'm going to let them keep the bonds — as a loan from you. An eighty-eight-thousand-dollar loan; they should be grateful to you. They will be, I think.

REGINA. (*Slowly, smiles.*) I see. You are punishing me. But I won't let you punish me. If you won't do anything, I will. Now. (*She starts for door.*)

HORACE. You won't do anything. Because you can't. (REGINA *stops.*) It won't do you any good to make trouble because I shall simply say that I lent them the bonds.

REGINA. (*Slowly*) You would do that?

HORACE. Yes. For once in your life I am tying your hands. There is nothing for you to do. (*There is silence. Then she sits down.*)

REGINA. I see. You are going to lend them the bonds and let them keep all the profit they make on them, and there is nothing I can do about it. Is that right?

HORACE. Yes.

REGINA. (*Softly*) Why did you say that I was making this gift?

HORACE. I was coming to that. I am going to make a new will, Regina, leaving you eighty-eight thousand dollars in Union Pacific bonds. The rest will go to Zan. It's true that your brothers have borrowed your share for a little while. After my death I advise you to talk to Ben and Oscar. They won't admit anything and Ben, I think, will be smart enough to see that he's safe. Because I knew about the theft and said nothing. Nor will I say anything as long as I live. Is that clear to you?

REGINA. (*Nods, softly, without looking at him.*) You will not say anything as long as you live.

HORACE. That's right. And by that time they will probably have replaced your bonds, and then they'll belong to you and nobody but us will ever know what happened. (*Stops, smiles.*) They'll be around any minute to see what I'm going to do. I took good care to see that word reached Leo. They'll be mighty relieved to know I'm going to do nothing and Ben will think it all a capital joke on you. And that will be the end of that. There's nothing you can do to them, nothing you can do to me.

REGINA. You hate me very much.

HORACE. No.

REGINA. Oh, I think you do. (*Puts her head back, sighs.*) Well, we haven't been very good together. Anyway, I don't hate you either. I have only contempt for you. I've always had.

HORACE. From the very first?

REGINA. I think so.

HORACE. I was in love with *you*. But why did *you* marry *me?*

REGINA. I was lonely when I was young.

HORACE. *You* were lonely?

REGINA. Not the way people usually mean. Lonely for all the things I wasn't going to get. Everybody in this house was so busy and there was so little place for what I wanted. I wanted the world. Then, and then — (*Smiles.*) Papa died and left the money to Ben and Oscar.

HORACE. And you married me?

REGINA. Yes, I thought — But I was wrong. You were a small-town clerk then. You haven't changed.

HORACE. (*Nods, smiles.*) And that wasn't what you wanted.

REGINA. No. No, it wasn't what I wanted. (*Pauses, leans back, pleasantly.*) It took me a little while to find out I had made a mistake. As for you — I don't know. It was almost as if I couldn't stand the kind of man you were — (*Smiles, softly.*) I used to lie there at night, praying you wouldn't come near —

HORACE. Really? It was as bad as that?

REGINA. (*Nods.*) Remember when I went to Doctor Sloan and I told you he said there was something the matter with me and that you shouldn't touch me any more?

HORACE. I remember.

REGINA. But you believed it. I couldn't understand that. I couldn't understand that anybody could be such a soft fool. That was when I began to despise you.

HORACE. (*Puts his hand to his throat, looks at the bottle of medicine on table.*) Why didn't you leave me?

REGINA. I told you I married you for something. It turned out it was only for this. (*Carefully*) This wasn't what I wanted, but it was something. I never thought about it much but if I had (HORACE *puts his hand to his throat.*) I'd have known that you would die before I would. But I couldn't have known that you would get heart trouble so early and so bad. I'm lucky, Horace. I've always been lucky. (HORACE *turns slowly to the medicine.*) I'll be lucky again. [*She watches him carefully, and with a certain air of triumph, as he reaches for the medicine.*]

[*Act III*]

HEDDA GABLER [22]

For 1 man; 1 woman

Henrik Ibsen

[*The scene is the* Tesmans' *villa, at Oslo. This is a spacious, handsome, and tastefully furnished drawing room; at the back, a wide doorway leading into a smaller room decorated in a similar style.* Judge Brack *has just brought to the* Tesman *household the news of* Eilert Lövborg's *attempted suicide.* Hedda's *husband* George *and* Mrs. Elvsted, *who has been devoted to* Lövborg, *have taken the latter's manuscript into the inner room, up center; they are prepared to see how much they can salvage of a book which "would have immortalized his name."* Hedda *crosses to an armchair near the stove down right; and presently* Brack *follows her.*]

Hedda. (*In a low voice*) Oh, what sense of freedom it gives one, this act of Eilert Lövborg's.

Brack. Freedom, Mrs. Hedda? Well, of course, it is a release for him —

Hedda. I mean for me. It gives me a sense of freedom to know that a deed of deliberate courage is still possible in this world — a deed of spontaneous beauty.

Brack. (*Smiling*) H'm — my dear Mrs. Hedda —

Hedda. Oh, I know what you are going to say. For you are a kind of a specialist too, like — you know!

Brack. (*Looking hard at her*) Eilert Lövborg was more to you than perhaps you are willing to admit to yourself. Am I wrong?

Hedda. I don't answer such questions. I only know that Eilert Lövborg has had the courage to live his life after his own fashion. And then — the last great act, with its beauty! Ah! that he should have the will and the strength to turn away from the banquet of life — so early.

Brack. I am sorry, Mrs. Hedda — but I fear I must dispel an amiable illusion.

Hedda. Illusion?

Brack. Which could not have lasted long in any case.

Hedda. What do you mean?

22 Trans. by Edmund Gosse and William Archer. Reprinted by permission of Charles Scribner's Sons, publishers.

BRACK. Eilert Lövborg did not shoot himself — voluntarily.

HEDDA. Not voluntarily?

BRACK. No. The thing did not happen exactly as I told it.

HEDDA. (*In suspense*) Have you concealed something? What is it?

BRACK. For poor Mrs. Elvsted's sake I idealized the facts a little.

HEDDA. What are the facts?

BRACK. First, that he is already dead.

HEDDA. At the hospital?

BRACK. Yes — without regaining consciousness.

HEDDA. What more have you concealed?

BRACK. This — the event did not happen at his lodgings.

HEDDA. Oh, that can make no difference.

BRACK. Perhaps it may. For I must tell you — Eilert Lövborg was found shot in — in Mademoiselle Diana's boudoir.

HEDDA. (*Makes a motion as if to rise, but sinks back again.*) That is impossible, Judge Brack! He cannot have been there again to-day.

BRACK. He was there this afternoon. He went there, he said, to demand the return of something which they had taken from him. Talked wildly about a lost child —

HEDDA. Ah — so that was why —

BRACK. I thought probably he meant his manuscript; but now I hear he destroyed that himself. So I suppose it must have been his pocket-book.

HEDDA. Yes, no doubt. And there — there he was found?

BRACK. Yes, there. With a pistol in his breast-pocket, discharged. The ball had lodged in a vital part.

HEDDA. In the breast — yes.

BRACK. No — in the bowels.

HEDDA. (*Looks up at him with an expression of loathing.*) That, too! Oh, what curse is it that makes everything I touch turn ludicrous and mean.

BRACK. There is one point more, Mrs. Hedda — another disagreeable feature in the affair.

HEDDA. And what is that?

BRACK. The pistol he carried —

HEDDA. (*Breathless*) Well? What of it?

BRACK. He must have stolen it.

HEDDA. (*Leaps up.*) Stolen it! That is not true! He did not steal it!

BRACK.   No other explanation is possible. He must have stolen it — Hush! . . . [BRACK *and* HEDDA *pause while* GEORGE *and* MRS. ELVSTED *re-arrange themselves, to afford better light for their work on the manuscript. After a while —*]

HEDDA.   (*Whispers*) What did you say about the pistol?

BRACK.   (*Softly*) That he must have stolen it.

HEDDA.   Why stolen it?

BRACK.   Because every other explanation ought to be impossible, Mrs. Hedda.

HEDDA.   Indeed?

BRACK.   (*Glances at her.*) Of course Eilert Lövborg was here this morning. Was he not?

HEDDA.   Yes.

BRACK.   Were you alone with him?

HEDDA.   Part of the time.

BRACK.   Did you not leave the room whilst he was here?

HEDDA.   No.

BRACK.   Try to recollect. Were you not out of the room a moment?

HEDDA.   Yes, perhaps just a moment — out in the hall.

BRACK.   And where was your pistol-case during that time?

HEDDA.   I had it locked up in —

BRACK.   Well, Mrs. Hedda?

HEDDA.   The case stood there on the writing-table.

BRACK.   Have you looked since, to see whether both the pistols are there?

HEDDA.   No.

BRACK.   Well, you need not. I saw the pistol found in Lövborg's pocket, and I knew it at once as the one I had seen yesterday — and before, too.

HEDDA.   Have you it with you?

BRACK.   No; the police have it.

HEDDA.   What will the police do with it?

BRACK.   Search till they find the owner.

HEDDA.   Do you think they will succeed?

BRACK.   (*Bends over her and whispers.*) No, Hedda Gabler — not so long as I say nothing.

HEDDA.   (*Looks frightened at him.*) And if you do not say nothing — what then?

BRACK.   (*Shrugs his shoulders.*) There is always the possibility that the pistol was stolen.

HEDDA. (*Firmly*) Death rather than that.

BRACK. (*Smiling*) People say such things — but they don't do them.

HEDDA. (*Without replying*) And supposing the pistol was stolen, and the owner is discovered? What then?

BRACK. Well, Hedda — then comes the scandal.

HEDDA. The scandal!

BRACK. Yes, the scandal — of which you are mortally afraid. You will, of course, be brought before the court — both you and Mademoiselle Diana. She will have to explain how the thing happened — whether it was an accidental shot or murder. Did the pistol go off as he was trying to take it out of his pocket, to threaten her with? Or did she tear the pistol out of his hand, shoot him, and push it back into his pocket? That would be quite like her; for she is an able-bodied young person, this same Mademoiselle Diana.

HEDDA. But *I* have nothing to do with all this repulsive business.

BRACK. No. But you will have to answer the question: Why did you give Eilert Lövborg the pistol? And what conclusions will people draw from the fact that you did give it to him?

HEDDA. (*Lets her head sink.*) That is true. I did not think of that.

BRACK. Well, fortunately, there is no danger, so long as I say nothing.

HEDDA. (*Looks up at him.*) So I am in your power, Judge Brack. You have me at your beck and call, from this time forward.

BRACK. (*Whispers softly.*) Dearest Hedda — believe me — I shall not abuse my advantage.

HEDDA. I am in your power none the less. Subject to your will and your demands. A slave, a slave, then! (*Rises impetuously.*) No, I cannot endure the thought of that! Never!

BRACK. (*Looks half-mockingly at her.*) People generally get used to the inevitable.

[*Act IV*]

THE DOVER ROAD [23]

For 1 man; 1 woman

A. A. MILNE

[NICHOLAS *and* EUSTASIA, *one of them already married (to some-one else), have "eloped," and have stopped at Mr. Latimer's house along the Dover Road. It is Mr. Latimer's intention that they shall have time to reconsider each other's character before proceeding with their plan to run away together, so he has arranged to keep them as his guests for a while. The scene is the reception room of Mr. Latimer's house.* NICHOLAS *and* EUSTASIA *have just finished breakfast, all during which* EUSTASIA *has been making what the author mildly calls a "gread deal of fuss" over* NICHOLAS.]

NICHOLAS.   Where are you going to sit? (*She goes to him, takes his hands, and puts him in settee and sits beside him — he R., she L.*)

EUSTASIA. (*Indicating the settee*) Nicholas sit there and Eustasia sit next to him.

NICHOLAS. (*Without much enthusiasm*) Right.

EUSTASIA. (*Snatches pouch.*) Eustasia fill his pipe for him?

NICHOLAS. (*He takes it back.*) No, thanks. It is filled, thank you. (*He lights his pipe. They are silent for a little, and at last he speaks, a little uncomfortably.*) Er, Eustasia.

EUSTASIA. Yes, darling.

NICHOLAS.   We've been here a week.

EUSTASIA. Yes, darling. A wonderful, wonderful week. And now today we leave this dear house where we have been so happy to-gether, and go out into the world together — (*Takes match from him and puts it on ash tray on mantel.*)

NICHOLAS. (*Who has not been listening to her*) A week. Except for the first day, we have had all our meals alone together.

EUSTASIA. (*Sentimentally*) Alone, Nicholas.

NICHOLAS.   Four meals a day. That's twenty-four meals.

EUSTASIA.   Twenty-four!

NICHOLAS.   And at every one of those meals you have asked me at least four times to have something more, when I had already said that I didn't want anything more; or, in other words, you have forced me to say "No, thank you, Eustasia," ninety-six times when there was absolutely no need of it.

[23] Reprinted by permission of the author and of G. P. Putnam's Sons.

EUSTASIA. (*Hurt*) Nicholas!

NICHOLAS. (*Inexorably*) We are both young. I am twenty-six, you are —

EUSTASIA. (*Quickly*) Twenty-five.

NICHOLAS. (*Looking at her and then away again*) You are twenty-five. If all goes well —(*sighs*) — we may look to have fifty more years together. Say two thousand five hundred weeks. Multiply that by a hundred, and we see that, in the course of our joint lives, you will, at the present rate, force me to say "No, thank you, Eustasia" two hundred and fifty thousand times more than is necessary.

EUSTASIA. (*Pathetically*) Nicholas!

NICHOLAS. (*Pipe in mouth*) I wondered if we couldn't come to some arrangement about it, that's all.

EUSTASIA. (*In tears*) You're cruel! Cruel! (*She sobs piteously, snatching his handkerchief.*)

NICHOLAS. (*Doggedly*) I just wondered if we couldn't come to some arrangement.

EUSTASIA. (*Completely overcome*) Oh! Oh! Nicholas! My darling! (*She sobs on end of couch.* NICHOLAS, *his hands clenched, looks grimly in front of him. He winces now and then at her sobs. He tries desperately hard not to give way, but in the end they are too much for him.*)

NICHOLAS. Darling! Don't! (*She goes on sobbing.*) There! There! I'm sorry. Nicholas is sorry. I oughtn't to have said it. Forgive me, darling. (*Her sobs get less.*)

EUSTASIA. (*Sitting up*) It's only because I love you so much, and w-want you to be well, and you m-must eat. (*Weeps.*)

NICHOLAS. Yes, yes, Eustasia, I know. It is dear of you.

EUSTASIA. Ask any doctor. He would say you m-must eat. (*Weeps.*)

NICHOLAS. Yes, darling.

EUSTASIA. You m-must eat. (*Weeps.*)

NICHOLAS. (*Resigned*) Yes, darling.

EUSTASIA. (*Sitting up and wiping her eyes*) What's a wife for, if it isn't to look after her husband when he's ill, and to see that he eats?

NICHOLAS. All right, dear, we won't say anything more about it.

EUSTASIA. And when you had that horrid cold and were so ill, the first day after we came here, I did look after you, didn't I, Nicholas, and take care of you and make you well again?

NICHOLAS. You did, dear. Don't think I am not grateful. You were very kind. (*Wincing at the recollection*) Too kind.

EUSTASIA. Not too kind, darling. I love looking after you, and taking care of you! (*Replaces handkerchief in his pocket. Thoughtfully, to herself*) Leonard was never ill.

NICHOLAS. Leonard?

EUSTASIA. My husband.

NICHOLAS. Oh! . . . I'd never thought of him as Leonard — I prefer not to think about him. I've never seen him, and I don't want to talk about him.

EUSTASIA. No, darling. I don't want to, either.

NICHOLAS. We've taken the plunge and — (*Bravely*) — and we're not going back on it.

EUSTASIA. (*Surprised*) Darling!

NICHOLAS. As a man of honor, I — Besides, you can't go back now — I mean, I took you away and — well, here we are (*Bravely*) — here we are.

EUSTASIA. (*Amazed*) Darling, you aren't regretting?

NICHOLAS. (*Hastily*) No, No! (*She again snatches his handkerchief.*) No, no, no!

EUSTASIA. Oh, yes, you are. (*Again sobs on end of couch.*)

NICHOLAS. No! No! (*He is almost shouting.*) Eustasia, listen! I love you! I'm not regretting! I've never been so happy! (*She is sobbing tumultuously.*) SO HAPPY, EUSTASIA! I . . . HAVE . . . NEVER . . . BEEN . . . SO . . . HAPPY! Can't you hear? (*Her sobs cease.*)

EUSTASIA. (*Thowing her arms round his neck — he subsides.*) Darling!

NICHOLAS. (*Comforting her*) There, there, there, there, there!

EUSTASIA. (*Drying her eyes*) Oh, Nicholas, you frightened me so. Just for a moment I was afraid you were regretting.

NICHOLAS. No, no!

EUSTASIA. (*Pause*) How right Mr. Latimer was! (*She is leaning affectionately on him.*)

NICHOLAS. (*With conviction*) He was, indeed.

EUSTASIA. How little we really knew of each other when you asked me to come away with you!

NICHOLAS. How little!

EUSTASIA. But this week has shown us to each other as we really are.

NICHOLAS. It has.

EUSTASIA. And now I feel absolutely safe. We are ready to face the world together, Nicholas. (*She sighs and leans back happily in his arms.*)

NICHOLAS. Ready to face the world together. (*He has his pipe in his left hand, which is round her waist. Her eyes are closed, her right hand encircling his neck. He tries to bend his head down so as to get hold of his pipe with his teeth. Several times he tries and just misses it. Each time he pulls her a little closer to him, and she sighs happily. At last he gets hold of it. He leans back with a sigh of relief — she also lies back.*)

[*Act II*]

ELIZABETH THE QUEEN [24]

For 1 man; 1 woman

MAXWELL ANDERSON

[*The queen's apartments in the Tower, a square and heavy room, long and with a raised stone platform at one end of which stands a regal chair. It is dawn, the light filtering in coldly.*

This is the last scene of the play. ELIZABETH *is seated on the royal chair.* ESSEX, *dressed in black and very pale, has just been admitted by a guard, who has retired.*]

ESSEX.   You sent for me?
          Or so they said.

ELIZABETH. Yes.

ESSEX.   It would have been kinder
          To leave me with my thoughts till the axe came down
          And ended them. You spoil me for death.

ELIZABETH. Are you
          So set on dying?

ESSEX.   I can't say I care for it.
          This blood that beats in us has a way of wanting
          To keep right on. But if one is to die
          It's well to go straight toward it.

24 Reprinted by permission of Longmans, Green & Co., Inc.

ELIZABETH.   You must have known
              I never meant you to die.

ESSEX.   I am under sentence
              From Your Majesty's courts. There's no appeal that I
                  know of.
              I am found guilty of treason on good evidence,
              And cannot deny it. This treason, I believe,
              Is punishable with death.

ELIZABETH.   God knows I am proud —
              And bitter, too — bitter at you with much cause,
              But I have sent for you. I've taken the first step
              That way. Do not make me take the next!

ESSEX.   The next is to the scaffold. It's only a step
              Now, and I've made ready. . . .

ELIZABETH.   You kept my ring. You never sent my ring.
              I've been waiting for it.

ESSEX.   You may have it back
              If you have use for it — I had thought to wear it
              As far as my grave, but, take it.

ELIZABETH.   I'd have forgiven
              All that had passed, at any hour, day or night,
              Since I last saw you. I have waited late at night
              Thinking, tonight the ring will come, he will never
              Hold out against me so long, but the nights went by
              Somehow, like the days, and it never came,
              Till the last day came, and here it is the last morning
              And the chimes beating out the hours.

ESSEX.   Dear, if I'd known —
              But I could not have sent it.

ELIZABETH.   Why?

ESSEX.   If I'd tried
              To hold you to a promise you could not keep
              And you had refused me, I should have died much
                  more
              Unhappy than I am now.

ELIZABETH.   I'd have kept my promise.
              I'd keep it now.

ESSEX.   If I offered you this ring?

ELIZABETH.   Yes — even now.

ESSEX.   You would pardon me, set me free,
Cede back my estates to me, love me as before,
Give me my place in the state?

ELIZABETH.   All as it was.

ESSEX.   And what would happen to your throne?

ELIZABETH.   My throne?
Nothing.

ESSEX.   Yes, for I'd take it from you.

ELIZABETH.   Again?
You'd play that game again?

ESSEX.   The games one plays
Are not the games one chooses always. I
Am still a popular idol of a sort.
There are mutterings over my imprisonment,
Even as it is — and if you should set me free
And confess your weakness by overlooking treason
And setting me up in power once more, the storm
That broke last time would be nothing to the storm
That would break over you then. As for myself,
I played for power and lost, but if I had
Another chance I think I'd play and win. . . .

ELIZABETH.   It cannot go this way!

ESSEX.   Aye, but it has.
It has and will. There's no way out. I've thought of it
Every way. Speak frankly. Could you forgive me
And keep your throne?

ELIZABETH.   No.

ESSEX.   Are you ready to give
Your crown up to me?

ELIZABETH.   No. It's all I have.
    (*She rises.*)
Why, who am I
To stand here paltering with a rebel noble!

I am Elizabeth, daughter of a king,
The queen of England, and you are my subject!
What does this mean, you standing here eye to eye
With me, your liege? You whom I made, and gave
All that you have, you, an upstart, defying
Me to grant pardon, lest you should sweep me from
    power
And take my place from me? I tell you if Christ his
    blood
Ran streaming from the heavens for a sign
That I should hold my hand you'd die for this,
You pretender to a throne upon which you have
No claim, you pretender to a heart, who have been
Hollow and heartless and faithless to the end!

ESSEX.   If we'd met some other how we might have been
              happy —
          But there's been an empire between us! I am to die —
          Let us say that — let us begin with that —
          For then I can tell you that if there'd been no empire
          We could have been great lovers. If even now
          You were not queen and I were not pretender,
          That god who searches heaven and earth and hell
          For two who are perfect lovers, could end his search
          With you and me. Remember — I am to die —
          And so I can tell you truly, out of all the earth
          That I'm to leave, there's nothing I'm very loath
          To leave save you. Yet if I live I'll be
          Your death or you'll be mine.

ELIZABETH.   Give me the ring.

ESSEX.   No.

ELIZABETH.   Give me the ring. I'd rather you killed me
              Than I killed you.

ESSEX.   It's better for me as it is
          Than that I should live and batten my fame and
              fortune
          On the woman I love. I've thought of it all. It's better
          To die young and unblemished than to live long and
              rule,
          And rule not well.

ELIZABETH.   Aye, I should know that.

ESSEX.   Is it not?

ELIZABETH.   Yes.

ESSEX.   Good-bye, then.

ELIZABETH.   Oh, then I'm old, I'm old!
I could be young with you, but now I'm old.
I know now how it will be without you. The sun
Will be empty and circle round an empty earth —
And I will be queen of emptiness and death —
Why could you not have loved me enough to give me
Your love and let me keep as I was?

ESSEX.   I know not.
I only know I could not. I must go.

ELIZABETH.   (*Frozen*)
Yes.
(*He goes to the door.*)
Lord Essex!
(*He turns.*)
Take my kingdom. It is yours!
[ESSEX, *as if not hearing, bows and goes on.*]
[ELIZABETH *bows her head.*]

[*Act III*]

PRIVATE LIVES [25]

For 1 man; 1 woman

NOEL COWARD

[*The scene is the terrace of a hotel in France; the time, a summer evening. Doors to separate suites appear up left and up right; and the terrace space is divided into two semi-private sections, each with suitable furnishings. Downstage, parallel to the footlights, is a low balustrade.*

ELYOT *and* AMANDA, *once married, are on their second honeymoon — this time with somebody else. Although they are trying to forget each other, they have had the misfortune of reserving adjoining suites at the same honeymoon hotel, where the orchestra has been playing a once-familiar and once-significant tune. For the moment they are alone on the terrace; they have just taken cocktails.*]

AMANDA. I tried to get away the moment after I'd seen you, but he wouldn't budge.

ELYOT. What's his name?

AMANDA. Victor, Victor Prynne.

ELYOT. (*Toasting*) Mr. and Mrs. Victor Prynne. (*He drinks.*) Mine wouldn't budge either.

AMANDA. What's her name?

ELYOT. Sibyl.

AMANDA. (*Toasting*) Mr. and Mrs. Elyot Chase. (*She drinks.*) God pity the poor girl.

ELYOT. Are you in love with him?

AMANDA. Of course.

ELYOT. How funny.

AMANDA. I don't see anything particularly funny about it, you're in love with yours, aren't you?

ELYOT. Certainly.

AMANDA. There you are then.

ELYOT. There we both are then.

AMANDA. What's she like?

ELYOT. Fair, very pretty, plays the piano beautifully.

AMANDA. Very comforting.

ELYOT. How's yours?

AMANDA. I don't want to discuss him.

ELYOT. Well, it doesn't matter, he'll probably come popping out in a minute and I shall see for myself. Does he know I'm here?

AMANDA. Yes, I told him.

ELYOT. (*With sarcasm*) That's going to make things a whole lot easier.

AMANDA. You needn't be frightened, he won't hurt you.

ELYOT. If he comes near me I'll scream the place down.

AMANDA. Does Sibyl know I'm here?

ELYOT. No, I pretended I'd had a presentiment. I tried terribly hard to persuade her to leave for Paris.

AMANDA. I tried too, it's lucky we didn't both succeed, isn't it? Otherwise we should probably all have joined up in Rouen or somewhere.

ELYOT. (*Laughing*) In some frowsy little hotel.

AMANDA. (*Laughing too*) Oh, dear, it would have been much, · much worse.

ELYOT. I can see us all sailing down in the morning for an early start.

AMANDA. (*Weakly*) Lovely, oh, lovely.

ELYOT. Glorious! (*They both laugh helplessly.*)

AMANDA. What's happened to yours?

ELYOT. Didn't you hear her screaming? She's downstairs in the dining-room, I think.

AMANDA. Mine is being grand, in the bar.

ELYOT. It really is awfully difficult.

AMANDA. Have you known her long?

ELYOT. About four months, we met in a house party in Norfolk.

AMANDA. Very flat, Norfolk.

ELYOT. How old is dear Victor?

AMANDA. Thirty-four, or -five; and Sibyl?

ELYOT. I blush to tell you, only twenty-three.

AMANDA. You've gone a mucker all right.

ELYOT. I shall reserve my opinion of your choice until I've met dear Victor.

AMANDA. I wish you wouldn't go on calling him "Dear Victor." It's extremely irritating.

ELYOT. That's how I see him. Dumpy, and fair, and very considerate, with glasses. Dear Victor.

AMANDA. As I said before I would rather not discuss him. At least I have good taste enough to refrain from making cheap gibes at Sibyl.

ELYOT. You said Norfolk was flat.

AMANDA. That was no reflection on her, unless she made it flatter.

ELYOT. Your voice takes on an acid quality whenever you mention her name.

AMANDA. I'll never mention it again.

ELYOT. Good, and I'll keep off Victor.

AMANDA. (*With dignity*) Thank you.

(*There is silence for a moment. The orchestra starts playing the same tune that they were singing previously.*)

ELYOT. That orchestra has a remarkably small repertoire.

AMANDA. They don't seem to know anything but this, do they? (*She sits down on the balustrade, and sings it, softly. Her eyes are looking out to sea, and her mind is far away.* ELYOT *watches her while she sings. When she turns to him at the end, there are tears in her eyes. He looks away awkwardly and lights another cigarette.*)

ELYOT. You always had a sweet voice, Amanda.

AMANDA. (*A little huskily*) Thank you.

ELYOT. I'm awfully sorry about all this, really I am. I wouldn't have had it happen for the world.

AMANDA. I know. I'm sorry too. It's just rotten luck.

ELYOT. I'll go away to-morrow whatever happens, so don't you worry.

AMANDA. That's nice of you.

ELYOT. I hope everything turns out splendidly for you, and that you'll be very happy.

AMANDA. I hope the same for you, too. (*The music, which has been playing continually through this little scene, returns persistently to the refrain. They both look at one another and laugh.*)

ELYOT. Nasty insistent little tune.

AMANDA. Extraordinary how potent cheap music is.

ELYOT. What exactly were you remembering at that moment?

AMANDA. The Palace Hotel Skating Rink in the morning, bright strong sunlight, and everybody whirling round in vivid colours, and you kneeling down to put on my skates for me.

ELYOT. You'd fallen on your fanny a few moments before.

AMANDA. It was beastly of you to laugh like that, I felt so humiliated.

ELYOT. Poor darling.

AMANDA. Do you remember waking up in the morning, and standing on the balcony, looking out across the valley?

ELYOT. Blue shadows on white snow, cleanness beyond belief, high above everything in the world. How beautiful it was.

AMANDA. It's nice to think we had a few marvelous moments.

ELYOT. A few? We had heaps really, only they slip away into the background, and one only remembers the bad ones.

AMANDA. Yes. What fools we were to ruin it all. What utter, utter fools.

ELYOT. You feel like that too, do you?

AMANDA. (*Wearily*) Of course.

ELYOT. Why did we?

AMANDA. The whole business was too much for us.

ELYOT. We were so ridiculously over in love.

AMANDA. Funny, wasn't it?

ELYOT. (*Sadly*) Horribly funny.

AMANDA. Selfishness, cruelty, hatred, possessiveness, petty jealousy. All those qualities came out in us just because we loved each other.

ELYOT. Perhaps they were there anyhow.

AMANDA. No, it's love that does it. To hell with love.

ELYOT. To hell with love.

AMANDA. And yet here we are starting afresh with two quite different people. In love all over again, aren't we? (ELYOT *doesn't answer.*) Aren't we?

ELYOT. No.

AMANDA. Elyot.

ELYOT. We're not in love all over again, and you know it. Goodnight, Amanda. (*He turns abruptly, and goes towards the French windows.*)

AMANDA. Elyot — don't be silly — come back.

ELYOT. I must go and find Sibyl.

AMANDA. I must go and find Victor.

ELYOT. (*Savagely*) Well, why don't you?

AMANDA. I don't want to.

ELYOT. It's shameful, shameful of us.

AMANDA. Don't: I feel terrible. Don't leave me for a minute, I shall go mad if you do. We won't talk about ourselves any more, we'll talk about outside things, anything you like, only just don't leave me until I've pulled myself together.

ELYOT. Very well. (*There is a dead silence.*)

AMANDA. What have you been doing lately? During these last years?

ELYOT. Travelling about. I went round the world, you know, after —

AMANDA. (*Hurriedly*) Yes, yes, I know. How was it?

ELYOT. The world?

AMANDA. Yes.

ELYOT. Oh, highly enjoyable.

AMANDA. China must be very interesting.

ELYOT. Very big, China.

AMANDA. And Japan —

ELYOT. Very small.

AMANDA. Did you eat sharks' fins, and take your shoes off, and use chopsticks and everything?

ELYOT. Practically everything.

AMANDA. And India, the burning Ghars, or Ghats, or whatever they are, and the Taj Mahal. How was the Taj Mahal?

ELYOT. (*Looking at her*) Unbelievable, a sort of dream.

AMANDA. That was the moonlight, I expect, you must have seen it in the moonlight.

ELYOT. (*Never taking his eyes off her face*) Yes, moonlight is cruelly deceptive.

AMANDA. And it didn't look like a biscuit box, did it? I've always felt that it might.

ELYOT. (*Quietly*) Darling, darling, I love you so.

AMANDA. And I do hope you met a sacred Elephant. They're lint white I believe, and very, very sweet.

ELYOT. I've never loved anyone else for an instant.

AMANDA. (*Raising her hand feebly in protest*) No, no, you mustn't — Elyot — stop.

ELYOT. You love me, too, don't you? There's no doubt about it anywhere, is there?

AMANDA. No, no doubt anywhere.

ELYOT. You're looking very lovely, you know, in this damned moonlight. Your skin is clear and cool, and your eyes are shining, and you're growing lovelier and lovelier every second as I look at you. You don't hold any mystery for me, darling, do you mind? There isn't a particle of you that I don't know, remember, and want.

AMANDA. (*Softly*) I'm glad, my sweet.

[*Act I*]

MILESTONES [26]

For 2 men

ARNOLD BENNETT and EDWARD KNOBLOCK

[*The time is 1860, the scene the drawing-room of the* RHEAD *house in Kensington Gore.* JOHN RHEAD *and* SAM SIBLEY *are partners in an iron company (with* SAM'S *father as third and senior partner).* JOHN *is forward-looking for his generation, and is considering entering the field of shipbuilding, though both his partners conservatively object.* JOHN *is in love with* ROSE SIBLEY, SAM'S *sister; and* SAM *is already engaged to marry* JOHN'S *sister,* GERTRUDE.

As the scene opens, JOHN *has just arranged for a few minutes
alone with* SAM SIBLEY.]

SAM. (*Suspicious, and not overfriendly*) What is it? Not business, I hope?

JOHN. (*With a successful effort to be cordial*) No, no!

SAM. (*Following* JOHN's *lead, and to make conversation*) I was
wondering what you and Rosie were palavering about.

JOHN. Samuel, you've gone right into the bull's-eye at the first
shot — Sam, I've just been through a very awkward moment. . . .

SAM. Am I right in assuming that Rose did not unconditionally
refuse your offer?

JOHN. She did me the honor to accept it.

SAM. I must confess I'm not entirely surprised that she didn't
spurn you.

JOHN. All right, old cock. Keep it up. I don't mind. But when
you're quite done, you might congratulate me.

SAM. (*Not effusively*) I do, of course. . . .

JOHN. Shake! (*They shake hands,* SAM *rather perfunctorily.*)
Now, Sam, I'm going to rely on you.

SAM. What for?

JOHN. I don't think you had any fault to find with my attitude
towards your engagement, had you? I welcomed it with both arms.
Well, I want you to do the same with me.

SAM. But, my dear fellow, I'm nobody in the affair. You're the
head of a family; I'm not.

JOHN. But you have enormous influence with the head of a family, my boy.

SAM. (*Rather falsely*) Why! Are you anticipating trouble with
the governor?

JOHN. I'm not anticipating it — but you know as well as I do —
probably much better — that he ain't very friendly disposed this
last day or two. The plain truth is — he's sulking. Now why?
Nothing whatever has passed between us except just every-day
business.

SAM. Well, the fact is, he suspects you're keeping something
nasty up your sleeve for him.

JOHN. Has he told you?

SAM. (*Rather pugnaciously*) Yes, he has.

JOHN. And what is it I'm supposed to have up my sleeve?

SAM. Look here, Jack. I'm not here to be cross-examined. If there's anything up your sleeve, you're the person to know what it is. It's not my sleeve we're talking about. Why don't you play with the cards on the table?

JOHN. I'm only too anxious to play with the cards on the table.

SAM. Then it is business you really wanted to talk about after all!

JOHN. (*Movement of irritation concealed*) I expect your father's heard about me and Macleans, though how it's got abroad I can't imagine.

SAM. Macleans? Macleans of Greenhithe? . . . By gad! I never dreamed you were hobnobbing with the Maclean gang.

JOHN. Macleans are one of the oldest shipbuilding firms in the South of England. I went to lunch today with Andrew Maclean.

SAM. What's ship-building got to do with us?

JOHN. It's got nearly everything to do with us. Or it will have. Now listen, Sammy. I've arranged a provisional agreement for partnership between Macleans and ourselves.

SAM. You've —

JOHN. Half a minute. Macleans are rather flattered at the idea of a connection with the august firm of Sibley, Rhead and Sibley.

SAM. By God! I should think they were. (*Walks away.*)

JOHN. They've had an output of over twenty-five thousand tons this year. All wood. Naturally they want to go in for iron. They'll pay handsomely for our help and experience. In fact, I've got a draft agreement, my boy, that is simply all in our favor.

SAM. Did you seriously suppose —

JOHN. Let me finish. It's a brilliant agreement. In three years it'll mean the doubling of our business. And we shall have the satisfaction of being well-established in the great industry of the future. . . .

SAM. And have you had the impudence to try to make an agreement behind our backs?

JOHN. (*Controlling himself*) I've made no agreement. I've only got the offer. It's open to you to refuse or accept. I only held my tongue about it so as to keep the job as easy as possible.

SAM. You had no right to approach anyone without consulting us.

JOHN. I was going to tell you tomorrow. . . . Come now, look at the thing calmly — reasonably. Don't condemn it offhand. A very great deal depends on your decision — more than you think.

SAM. I don't see that anything particular depends on my decision. If we refuse, we refuse. And we shall most decidedly refuse.

JOHN. But it's impossible you should be so blind to the future! Impossible!

SAM. See here, John! Don't you make the mistake of assuming that any man who doesn't happen to agree with you is a blind fool. . . . Don't you go and imagine that all the arguments are on one side. They aren't. Five-sixths of the experts in England have no belief .whatever in the future of iron ships. You know that! Iron ships indeed! And what about British oak? Would you build ships of the self-same material as bridges? Why not stone ships, then? Oh, yes, I know there's a number of faddists up and down the land — anything in the nature of a novelty is always bound to attract a certain type of brain. Unfortunately we happen to have that type of brain just now in the Cabinet. I quite agree with my father that the country is going to the dogs. Another Reform Bill this year! And actually an attempt to repeal the paper duty. But, of course, people who believe in iron ships would naturally want to unsettle the industrial classes by a poisonous flood of cheap newspapers! However, we've had enough common-sense left to knock both those schemes on the head. And I've no doubt the sagacity of the country will soon also put an end to this fantastic notion of iron ships.

JOHN. (*Quietly*) I see.

SAM. Oh, don't think I'm not fond of iron! Iron means as much to me as it does to you. But I flatter myself I can keep my balance. (*More quietly*) We didn't expect this of you, John, with your intellect.

JOHN. (*As before*) Very well.

SAM. I've made it clear, haven't I?

JOHN. Quite.

SAM. That's all right.

JOHN. (*Still quietly*) Only I shall dissolve partnership.

SAM. Dissolve partnership? What for?

JOHN. I shall go on with Macleans alone.

SAM. You don't mean it.

JOHN. I mean every single word of it! (*He rises. They look at each other.*)

SAM. Then I can tell you one thing. You won't marry Rosie.

JOHN. Why shan't I marry Rosie?

SAM. After such treachery.

JOHN. (*Raising his voice*) Treachery! I merely keep my own opinion — I leave you to yours.

SAM. Do you think father will let you drag Rosie into this fatuous scheme of yours? Do you think he'll give his daughter to a traitor?

JOHN. (*Sarcastic and cold*) Don't get on stilts. (*Then suddenly bursting out*) And what has my marriage got to do with you? When I want your father's opinion, I'll go to your father for it.

SAM. Don't try to browbeat me, John. I know my father's mind, and what's more, you know I know it. And I repeat, my father will never let his daughter marry a —

JOHN. (*Shouting*) Silence!

[*Act I*]

ESCAPE [27]

For 2 men

JOHN GALSWORTHY

[*Dartmeet. An open space of fern and grass, above the river and away from trippers.*

MATT, *who has been working along the river all the morning, is squatting with his catch beside him — some eight smallish trout. He is eating the last of his chocolate and drinking diligently from the already empty flask. The more so as an* OLD GENTLEMAN *in Lovat tweeds is straying towards him.* MATT *begins taking his rod to pieces.*

Seven hours have passed since MATT DENANT *has escaped from the prison farm at Dartmoor.*]

OLD GENTLEMAN. (*Approaching from Left*) Afternoon! Cleared up too well for *you*, I'm afraid.

MATT. Yes, it's a bit bright now.

OLD GENTLEMAN. Best eating in the world, those little brown chaps. Except perhaps the blue trout in the Tirol. *Blaue Forellen* with butter and potatoes, and a bottle of Vöslauer Goldeck, eh?

MATT. My Golly, yes! (*He looks wolfishly at his trout.*)

OLD GENTLEMAN. (*Eyeing him askance*) Very foggy this morning. Worst point about the moor, these fogs. Only good for convicts — um?

[27] Reprinted by permission of Charles Scribner's Sons, publishers.

MATT. (*Subduing a start*) Escapes, you mean? But they never get clear, I believe.

OLD GENTLEMAN. No, I'm told; but they try, you know — they try. I've often wondered what I should do if I blundered into an escaped convict.

MATT. Yes, sir; bit of a problem.

OLD GENTLEMAN. (*Sitting down on his overcoat*) Between the Law and one's gentlemanly instincts — if it's gentlemanlike to dally with a felon — I wonder!

MATT. (*Warming to the subject*) A chap who tries to escape must be a sportsman, anyway. He takes a pretty long chance.

OLD GENTLEMAN. Yes, I don't envy a man in this country; we're a law-abiding people. I remember being very much struck with the difference in America last year — vital race, that — sublime disregard of the law themselves, and a strong sense of moral turpitude in others. Been in America?

MATT. I was out West ranching when the war broke out.

OLD GENTLEMAN. Indeed! Judging by the films, escaping justice is still fashionable there. I think I prefer a more settled country.

MATT. Personally, I've got rather a complex. Escaped from Germany in the war.

OLD GENTLEMAN. Did you? How very interesting!

MATT. If you want to get thin. It's a top-hole cure for adipose. An escape's no picnic.

OLD GENTLEMAN. I imagine not, indeed. Where did you get over the border?

MATT. Holland, after three days and nights on beets and turnips. Do you know the turnip in a state of nature, Sir? He's a homely fellow — only beaten by the beet. Beg your pardon, Sir, it slipped out. By the way, a convict got off the day before yesterday.

OLD GENTLEMAN. Yes, I saw that — a Captain Matt Denant. I read his case with interest at the time. How did it strike you?

MATT. (*On guard*) Don't believe I remember it.

OLD GENTLEMAN. What? The Hyde Park case!

MATT. Oh! Ah! yes. There was a girl. In those cases they might wait till you complain.

OLD GENTLEMAN. The detective was undoubtedly doing his duty. And yet, quite a question — Rather dangerous giving the police a discretion on morals. The police are very like ourselves; and — er — most of us haven't got discretion, and the rest haven't got morals.

The young man didn't complain, I think. D'you happen to recollect?

MATT. (*With an uneasy look*) So far as I remember, he said she was an intellectual.

(*The* OLD GENTLEMAN *has taken out a cigar-case and is offering it.*)

OLD GENTLEMAN. Smoke?

MATT. Thanks very much. I've got into a bad habit of coming out without tobacco.

(*They bite and light cigars.*)

OLD GENTLEMAN. I suppose one might run across that convict fellow any moment. It would be a little like meeting an adder. The poor thing only wants to get away from you. And yet, if you don't break its back, ten to one it'll bite a dog. I had two dogs die of snakebite. It's a duty, perhaps — what do you say?

MATT. Probably. But I don't always do mine.

OLD GENTLEMAN. Oh! don't you? I'm so glad of that. Neither do I.

MATT. Do you know that Prison? It's a bad style of architecture.

OLD GENTLEMAN. No. The fact is, I've had the misfortune in my time to send a good many people to prison. And in those days I did make a point of seeing a prison now and then. I remember I used to give my Juries a pass to go and see where they sent their fellow-beings. Once I tested whether they went to look round or not, and out of three Juries — no, it was four — how many do you think had had the curiosity?

MATT. None.

OLD GENTLEMAN. Isn't that a little cynical? (*With his sideway bird-like glance*) No, it was — one. Ha!

MATT. Who'd want to go into a prison? I'd as soon visit the morgue. The bodies there aren't *living*, anyway.

OLD GENTLEMAN. They tell me prisons are much improved. They've introduced a human feeling.

MATT. Have they? Splendid! What was the date of that?

OLD GENTLEMAN. (*His eyes busy*) They've abolished the arrows, anyway. And I believe they don't shave their heads now. Do you know any convicts?

MATT. (*With a wriggle*) I? No. Only one.

OLD GENTLEMAN. Indeed? And is he interesting?

MATT. The most interesting chap I know.

OLD GENTLEMAN. Ha! Suppose this escaped convict suddenly turned up here? (*Jerking his thumb towards* MATT) What should you do?

MATT. Run like a hare.

OLD GENTLEMAN. Dear me, yes. I think it would depend on whether anyone was about. Human nature is very — er — sensitive. D'you find this climate bracing? Dartmoor has quite a reputation.

MATT. Overrated — I think.

OLD GENTLEMAN. You know it well?

MATT. No; this is my first visit.

OLD GENTLEMAN. And will you be here long?

MATT. Hope not.

OLD GENTLEMAN. Beautiful spot — Dartmeet!

MATT. I prefer Two Bridges. (*Putting up his rod and whistling* "*Lady, be good*")

OLD GENTLEMAN. Ah! What fly have you been using?

MATT. Just a tag.

OLD GENTLEMAN. I've not fished for years. (*As* MATT *suddenly passes his hand over his brow under his hat*) Anything the matter?

MATT. Afraid I shall have to abandon your excellent cigar. I've enjoyed it, but I'm smoking on a rather empty stomach. (*He looks ruefully at the unsmoked portion of his cigar, and pitches it away.*)

OLD GENTLEMAN. Dear me! Yes. I remember that feeling coming over me once at the Royal Academy banquet — just before I had to make a speech. (*Another of his bird-like glances*) Tobacco must be one of the great deprivations in prison, I always think. Didn't you find that so in — in — Germany?

MATT. (*Breathing rather fast and completing the dismantlement of his fishing rod.*) Oh! we got tobacco now and then.

OLD GENTLEMAN. And empty stomachs too, I'm afraid.

MATT. Yes.

OLD GENTLEMAN. One never ceases to be grateful to those who endured such things. (*Offering his cigar-case*) Will you try again after tea? These moor teas with cream and jam.

MATT. (*Taking it*) Well, thank you, Sir. I shall down him next time. (MATT *is now ready for departure for he has been getting increasingly uneasy with this* OLD GENTLEMAN. *He takes up his basket and lays the fish within it.*)

OLD GENTLEMAN. Well, (*Getting up*) I must be getting on too. It's been very pleasant. I've enjoyed our little talk. At my time of life one doesn't often get new sensations.

MATT. (*Nonplussed*) Good Lord, Sir! Have I given you any?

OLD GENTLEMAN. Well, I don't remember ever having talked before to a prisoner who'd escaped from — Germany.

MATT. Good-bye, Sir.

OLD GENTLEMAN. Good-bye, Captain Denant — (MATT *starts.*) I hope you'll have a pleasant journey, especially as no one seems to have noticed our little chat.

MATT. (*Staring at him*) D'you mind frightfully telling me how you spotted me?

OLD GENTLEMAN. Not at all! First, the way you looked at your trout — shall I say — er — wolfishly? And then — forgive me — your legs.

MATT. (*Drawing up his Burberry and contemplating his legs*) Yes. I hoped you'd think I was a leader of fashion.

OLD GENTLEMAN. And there was another thing — your obvious sympathy with yourself.

MATT. That's a prison habit, Sir. You're not allowed to sympathize with other people, for fear of contaminating them. Before I got into quod I don't remember ever feeling sorry for myself. But I doubt if I shall ever again feel sorry for anyone else.

OLD GENTLEMAN. That must be very natural. Well, it's been most interesting, because now you see I know what I should do —

MATT. (*Intently*) Is it indiscreet to ask, Sir?

OLD GENTLEMAN. Well, Captain Denant, this time — I say *this* time — wink the other eye. Good-day to you!

MATT. Good-day, Sir. It's most frightfully sporting of you. For the moment I feel quite human.

OLD GENTLEMAN. Do you know, that's been rather the effect on me. Original sin, I suppose. Good-day!

(*He goes off, watching the smoke of his cigar and smiling faintly to himself. On* MATT, *affected by kindness*

THE CURTAIN FALLS)

[Part II, Episode iv]

MARY OF SCOTLAND [28]

For 2 women

MAXWELL ANDERSON

[*The scene is a prison room in Carlisle Castle, in England. After years of scheming,* QUEEN ELIZABETH *now holds* MARY *prisoner, offering her freedom only if she will abdicate her throne. The room is scantily furnished; there are two windows at the right, both barred, a window at center rear, and a hall door at the left.*]

MARY.　How could I have been
Mistaken in you for an instant?

ELIZABETH.　You were not mistaken.
I am all women I must be. One's a young girl,
Young and harrowed as you are — one who could weep
To see you here — and one's a bitterness
At what I've lost and can never have, and one's
The basilisk you saw. This last stands guard
And I obey it. Lady, you came to Scotland
A fixed and subtle enemy, more dangerous
To me than you've ever known. This could not be borne,
And I set myself to cull you out and down,
And down you are.

MARY.　When was I your enemy?

ELIZABETH.　Your life was a threat to mine, your throne to my throne,
Your policy a threat.

MARY.　How? Why?

ELIZABETH.　It was you
Or I. Do you know that? The one of us must win
And I must always win. Suppose one lad
With a knife in his hand, a Romish lad who planted
That knife between my shoulders — my kingdom was yours.

[28] From *Mary of Scotland*, by Maxwell Anderson, copyright, 1933. Reprinted by permission of Doubleday & Company, Inc.

	It was too easy. You might not have wished it, But you'd take it if it came.
MARY.	And you'd take my life And love to avoid this threat?
ELIZABETH.	Nay, keep your life. And your love, too. The lords have brought a parch- ment For you to sign. Sign it and live.
MARY.	If I sign it Do I live where I please? Go free?
ELIZABETH.	Nay, I would you might, But you'd go to Bothwell, and between you two You might be too much for Moray. You'll live with me In London. There are other loves, my dear. You'll find amusement there in the court. I assure you It's better than a cell.
MARY.	And if I will not sign This abdication?
ELIZABETH.	You've tasted prison. Try A diet of it.
MARY.	And so I will.
ELIZABETH.	I can wait.
MARY.	And I can wait. I can wait better than you. Bothwell will fight free again. Kirkaldy Will fight beside him, and others will spring up From these dragon's teeth you've sown. Each week that passes I'll be stronger, and Moray weaker.
ELIZABETH.	And do you fancy They'll rescue you from an English prison? Why, Let them try it.
MARY.	Even that they may do. I wait for Bothwell — And wait for him here.
ELIZABETH.	Where you will wait, bear in mind, Is for me to say. Give up Bothwell, give up your throne If you'd have a life worth living.

MARY.   I will not.

ELIZABETH.   I can wait.

MARY.   And will not because you play to lose. This trespass
               Against God's right will be known. The nations will
                 know it,
               Mine and yours. They will see you as I see you
               And pull you down.

ELIZABETH.   Child, child, I've studied this gambit
               Before I play it. I will send each year
               This paper to you. Not signing, you will step
               From one cell to another, step lower always,
               Till you reach the last, forgotten, forgotten of men,
               Forgotten among causes, a wraith that cries
               To fallen gods in another generation
               That's lost your name. Wait then for Bothwell's
                 rescue.
               It will never come.

MARY.   I may never see him?

ELIZABETH.   Never.
               It would not be wise.

MARY.   And suppose indeed you won
               Within our lifetime, still, looking down from the
                 heavens
               And up from men around us, God's spies that watch
               The fall of great and little, they will find you out —
               I will wait for that, wait longer than a life,
               Till men and the times unscroll you, study the tricks
               You play, and laugh, as I shall laugh, being known
               Your better, haunted by your demon, driven
               To death or exile by you, unjustly. Why,
               When all's done, it's my name I care for, my name
                 and heart,
               To keep them clean. Win now, take your triumph
                 now,
               For I'll win men's hearts in the end — though the sift-
                 ing takes
               This hundred years — or a thousand.

ELIZABETH.   Child, child, are you gulled
               By what men write in histories, this or that,

And never true? I am careful of my name
As you are, for this day and longer. It's not what
    happens
That matters, no, not even what happens that's true,
But what men believe to have happened. They will
    believe
The worst of you, the best of me, and that
Will be true of you and me. I have seen to this.
What will be said about us in after-years
By men to come, I control that, being who I am.
It will be said of me that I governed well,
And wisely, but of you, cousin, that your life,
Shot through with ill-loves, battened on lechery, made
    you
An ensign of evil, that men tore down and trampled.
Shall I call for the lords' parchment?

MARY. This will be said — ?
But who will say it? It's a lie — will be known as a lie!

ELIZABETH. You lived with Bothwell before Darnley died,
You and Bothwell murdered Darnley.

MARY. And that's a lie!

ELIZABETH. Your letters, my dear. Your letters to Bothwell prove
    it.
We have those letters.

MARY. Then they're forged and false!
For I never wrote them!

ELIZABETH. It may be they were forged.
But will that matter, Mary, if they're believed?
All history is forged.

MARY. You would do this?

ELIZABETH. It is already done.

MARY. And still I win.
A demon has no children, and you have none,
Will have none, can have none, perhaps. This crooked
    track
You've drawn me on, cover it, let it not be believed
That a woman was a fiend. Yes, cover it deep,

And heap my infamy over it, lest men peer
And catch sight of you as you were and are. In myself
I know you to be an eater of dust. Leave me here
And set me lower this year by year, as you promise,
Till the last is an oubliette, and my name inscribed
On the four winds. Still, STILL I win! I have been
A woman, and I have loved as a woman loves,
Lost as a woman loses. I have borne a son,
And he will rule Scotland — and England. You have
    no heir!
A devil has no children.

ELIZABETH.   By God, you shall suffer
For this, but slowly.

MARY.   And that I can do. A woman
Can do that. Come, turn the key. I have a hell
For you in mind, where you will burn and feel it,
Live where you like, and softly.

ELIZABETH.   Once more I ask you,
And patiently. Give up your throne.

MARY.   No, devil.
My pride is stronger than yours, and my heart beats
    blood
Such as yours has never known. And in this dungeon,
I win here, alone.

ELIZABETH.   (*Turning*) Good-night, then.

MARY.   Aye, good-night.
(ELIZABETH *goes to the door. She goes out slowly.
As the door begins to close upon her* MARY *calls:*)
Beaton!

ELIZABETH.   (*Turning*) You will not see your maids again,
I think. It's said they bring you news from the north.

MARY.   I thank you for all kindness.
(ELIZABETH *goes out.* MARY *stands for a moment in
thought, then walks to the wall and lays her hand
against the stone, pushing outward. The stone is cold,
and she shudders. Going to the window, she sits
again in her old place and looks out into the darkness.*)
[*Act III*]

LADIES IN RETIREMENT [29]

For 2 women

EDWARD PERCY and REGINALD DENHAM

[*The scene is the living-room of Miss Fiske's pre-Tudor farm-house in the Thames marshes.* LEONORA FISKE *is described as a "retired lady of easy virtue," who has chosen to spend the last years of her life in rural retirement; and she occupies Estuary House with her friend and housekeeper-companion,* ELLEN CREED. LEONORA *is a good-hearted woman with a shrewd sense of wit and a rather quick temper.*

ELLEN *is a tall, striking-looking woman, with considerable dignity and a deep family sense. Her two slightly addled sisters have been visiting Estuary House, and have begun to get on* LEONORA'S *nerves. The present scene has been preceded by a particularly annoying incident.*]

LEONORA. (*Crosses R.C.*) I'm sorry I was so put out, Ellen. But there's a limit to patience, you know.

ELLEN. It's I who should have apologized.

LEONORA. Nonsense, dear. I mustn't expect you to be responsible for your sisters.

ELLEN. But I am responsible for them. . . . They have been a little naughty today, I admit. (*Crosses to stairs.*) But I'll give them a good talking to, and then everything will be all right.

LEONORA. (*Firmly*) That won't do, Ellen. I'm trying to tell you, as kindly as I can, that they've got to go.

ELLEN. (*She seems stunned.*) To go? When? (*There is a pause.*) When do you want them to go?

LEONORA. At once. This week. I can't stand them any longer. I'm at the end of my tether.

ELLEN. (*Crosses to table C.*) I don't know how I shall break it to them.

LEONORA. (*Growing exasperated*) But I only invited them here for a few weeks. Didn't they understand that? They've been here nearly four months.

ELLEN. Oh, no! Surely not as long as that?

LEONORA. They came at the beginning of June, and now we're well into September. And another thing. (*Crosses to* ELLEN.) I don't think you've been quite fair to me. You never told me they were — well, what they are.

ELLEN. I told you they were rather pathetic.

LEONORA. Yes, my dear; but pathetic's not next door to insane.

ELLEN. (*Almost savagely*) They're not insane!

LEONORA. Naturally, you put the best side of the picture forward. They're your own flesh and blood. But, insane or pathetic or whatever you choose to call them, they've overstayed their welcome. I won't have them here any longer. (*Crosses with polish and duster, puts them on landing.*)

ELLEN. It's your house, I know. But you'll have to give me a little time.

LEONORA. What's time got to do with it?

ELLEN. Well, I don't quite know where I'll be able to send them.

LEONORA. (*Crosses down from landing.*) But surely they've only got to get into a train and go back where they came from?

ELLEN. No. I didn't keep on their room.

LEONORA. (*Crosses to* ELLEN.) But, my dear! You knew they weren't coming here on a visit for life!

ELLEN. I didn't want the expense. Besides, I hoped that perhaps you might have taken to them more than you have. I hoped we might be able to arrange something. It's a large house. There are several empty rooms. I was going to suggest that I should pay you something out of my wages toward their keep. . . . I admit I didn't realize quite how you felt. You've never given an inkling of it.

LEONORA. My dear Ellen, are you quite blind? You must have seen that I've got more and more exasperated.

ELLEN. I thought we might have gone on as we were for a little longer.

LEONORA. Well, you know how I feel now. I hope you realize we can't. This little holiday has come to an end. (*Crosses to piano.*)

ELLEN. (*Sits R. of table.*) You make me feel my position very much. I suppose you want me to go, too?

LEONORA. My dear Ellen, of course not! We got on like a house on fire before they came. I don't regard you, dear, as my servant, I think of you as my friend. You know my pillar-to-post career hasn't made me any permanent ones. Mine's a lonely existence. Terribly lonely. It's bound to be. And I've no family — no relations to fall back on. (*Crosses to above table.*) So, you see, I value your companionship. More, perhaps, than you realize. I definitely don't want you to go.

ELLEN. (*Rises, crosses to sofa D.R.*) I'm afraid it won't be altogether easy to forget what you think about my sisters. Or that you turned them out when they were so happy.

LEONORA. (*Crosses to* ELLEN.) But I haven't turned them out! Their visit's just come to its end in the normal way. That's all.

ELLEN. Things can never be quite the same, can they?

LEONORA. Ellen! Don't tell me that you're crazy, too! For goodness' sake, try to see this thing sensibly. Don't you realize that you're being frightfully unreasonable?

ELLEN. (*Sits on sofa.*) People who've got all they want never understand how much the smallest thing means to those who haven't.

LEONORA. (*Getting very angry*) Really! I don't think this calls for a sermon on charity! I've been more than generous to you and your sisters.

ELLEN. But it's a little cruel to give with one hand only to take away with the other.

LEONORA. Oh, my goodness! You're beginning to make me wish I'd never given at all! (*Crosses C.*)

ELLEN. People have always been very generous to you, Leonora. You've got a home. You've got investments. You've got your one or two — allowances, haven't you?

LEONORA. Well, what of it? (*Crosses U.L., paces about the room.*)

ELLEN. My sisters and I — we haven't any gentlemen to send us money.

LEONORA. That's hardly my fault, is it?

ELLEN. No, but don't you ever feel that you have a special responsibility to women like us?

LEONORA. (*Still moving about*) I don't know what you're talking about!

ELLEN. Don't you owe a debt to virtue? I've had to work for the money I've made. But at least I've kept my self-respect.

LEONORA. (*Raging. Crosses R. to* ELLEN.) How dare you? How dare you criticize my life? Do you think it hasn't been slavery to get the little I've got? Do you think it's cost me nothing but a few cheap embraces? How can you, a dried-up old spinster — how can

you understand anything of what my life's been? Do you think I
haven't had my torments? Do you think I don't envy women who've
got respectability, who've got families, who aren't just forgotten or
pensioned off when they lose their stock-in-trade?

ELLEN. Then you can't blame me for fighting for my family!

LEONORA. Ellen, you're a hypocrite. You're worse. You're a
cheat. You've pretended to be my friend. But it wasn't friendship
you felt for me. You meant to batten on me and get the utmost
out of me. You wanted to foist your wretched brood on me in-
definitely. You wanted to manoeuvre me into a false position and
bleed me white. And when I saw through your little scheme you
had the insolence to turn on me and abuse me. But you've chosen
the wrong woman! (*Going to the kitchen door*) I suggest you take
a month's wages and go. (*She stands looking at the seated* ELLEN.
She is shaking with rage. Then to her amazement ELLEN *crumples
up. She bursts into tears.*)

ELLEN. Leonora, don't go like that. Don't go, please. I'm absolutely in the wrong. I didn't mean half I said. I'm dreadfully sorry.

LEONORA. (*Still quivering*) I should hope you are!

ELLEN. You're quite right about my sisters. They are — peculiar.
I don't wonder they've got on your nerves. I think perhaps they've
got on mine, too, and that's why I said what I did. But, you see, I
love them. I love them intensely — just because they are so help-
less. They're almost a religion with me. You're quite right, though,
Leonora. They can't stay here. They must go. I see that. Only
don't send me away, too. I've been so happy here. And I promise
everything shall be the same as before. Only don't send me away.

(LEONORA *moved but still hurt*)

LEONORA. Well, I think we'd better both sleep on it, Ellen.
(*Then she goes quietly and quickly out into the kitchen.*)

[*Act I, Scene ii*]

Index to Selections

★★★ _____ ★★★

Index to Subject Matter